THE GIFT OF DIALOGUE

THE ENCYCLICAL ECCLESIAM SUAM AND THE KEY DOCUMENTS OF VATICAN II ON INTERRELIGIOUS DIALOGUE AND ECUMENISM

INTRODUCTION BY ARCHBISHOP KEVIN MCDONALD

All documents are published thanks to the generous support of the members of the Catholic Truth Society

CATHOLIC TRUTH SOCIETY
PUBLISHERS TO THE HOLY SEE

ISBN 978 1 86082 931 4

CONTENTS

INTRODUCTION

The fiftieth anniversary of the Second Vatican Council is being marked throughout the world by many conferences, lectures and publications. As well as remembering and celebrating the actual event of the Council, attention is being paid to the individual Constitutions, Decrees and Declarations that make up the Council's body of teaching.

This volume comprises three documents. Two of them are key texts of the Council which have had a defining effect on the role and profile of the Catholic Church in the world of today. They are the Decree on Ecumenism, *Unitatis Redintegratio* and the Declaration on Non-Christian Religions, *Nostra Aetate*. The third and much the longest of the three texts, is not a Council document but, rather, an encyclical written during the Council by Pope Paul VI. It was and remains a vitally important document since it sets out the context and the significance of the two other documents which precede it in this booklet.

It is well known that for those people who rejected Vatican II the two Council documents published here were a particular problem. Both were seen as constituting innovation which had no foundation in previous Church teaching. There has subsequently been much discussion of the question of continuity and discontinuity in the teaching of Vatican II. In fact, its teaching clearly encompasses both of those things as was acknowledged in some succinct comments on this debate by Pope Benedict:

"It is precisely in this combination of continuity and discontinuity at different levels that the very nature of true reform consists...The Second Vatican Council with its new definition of the relationship between the faith of the Church and certain elements of modern thought, has reviewed or even corrected certain historical decisions, but in this apparent discontinuity, it has actually preserved and deepened her inmost nature and true identity." (*Address to the Roman Curia,* 22nd December, 2005)

So it is precisely the interplay of continuity and discontinuity in the teaching of Vatican II that secures true development in teaching and effectively frees the Church to be more fully itself.

The Council's teaching on other religions draws on Scripture, the teaching of the Fathers and key theologians of the twentieth century, in such a way as to put the Church into a new relationship with Judaism and with other religions too. Surprisingly perhaps it is in the field of ecumenism that the dynamics of change and development can seem most remarkable. Ever since the start of the modern ecumenical movement at the beginning of the twentieth century, the Church had tended to stress the problems and dangers of ecumenism. At Vatican II it drew on Scripture and Tradition to set out a positive and theologically-grounded vision of other Churches and Ecclesial Communities. The Council's teaching did this in such a way that ecumenical dialogue which seeks to establish ever-fuller communion between separated Christians became central to the mission and, indeed, the identity of the Catholic Church.

So the two conciliar texts reprinted here have significantly shaped the role and profile of the Church in the years since the Council. It is important to remember, however, that the documents on ecumenism and on other religions can only be appreciated and understood if they are seen as an integral part of the teaching of the Council as a whole. The Council texts are mutually illuminating and of particular relevance here is the Dogmatic Constitution on the Church, *Lumen Gentium*. Its opening paragraph states that "The Church exists in Christ as a sacrament or instrumental sign of intimate union with God and of unity for the whole human race." The most significant conciliar teaching on ecumenism and on other religions is actually to be found in the second chapter of *Lumen Gentium,* entitled The People of God. This chapter presents a panoramic and inclusive vision of the Church. It speaks of other Christians, the Jews, members of other religions and, indeed, all people of good will as being in some way ordered to the one People of God. This powerful vision of the unity of all humanity is also explored in the Pastoral Constitution on the Church in the Modern World which affirms that "the Holy Spirit offers to all, the possibility of being made partners, in a way known to God, in the paschal mystery."(*Gaudium et Spes,* 22) The point is that the two conciliar documents published here are essentially teaching documents about the nature of the Church.

What is remarkable about these two texts is that they are very short and therefore left many questions unanswered. To take the work forward, after the Council Pope Paul created two Secretariats as permanent offices of the Roman Curia. These would eventually become the Pontifical Council for Promoting Christian Unity and the Pontifical Council for Interreligious Dialogue. He also founded the Commission for Religious Relations with the Jews, an office which is housed within the Pontifical Council for Promoting Christian Unity. All three offices have done a huge amount of work in promoting and developing the conciliar teaching that brought them into being. The promoting and developing of this dimension of the Church's outreach also became a central feature of the office of the Pope. The event that focuses most clearly the way in which this teaching developed the office of the papacy was the Prayer for Peace in Assisi in 1986 when St John Paul II gathered together other Christian leaders and leaders of other religions to pray and witness to peace together. He afterwards affirmed that through this event the Church came to a deeper understanding of its own identity. (*Address to the Roman Curia,* December 1986)

Bishops' Conferences have also sought to take this work forward and it is appropriate in this context to mention two documents of the Bishops' Conference of England and Wales which have sought to apply the conciliar teaching to the situation in this country. On ecumenism, there was the document *One Bread One Body,* published in 1998 and on interreligious dialogue there was *Meeting God in Friend and Stranger,* in 2010.

Pope Paul's encyclical *Ecclesiam Suam,* was published in 1964 and was clearly intended to shape and guide the work of the Council. It is hard to overstate the importance of this document since it provides the key to understanding the commitment to ecumenical and interreligious dialogue in the contemporary Catholic Church. Section 70 says this:

"Here, then, Venerable Brethren, is the noble origin of this dialogue: in the mind of God himself. Religion of its very nature is a certain relationship between God and man. It finds its expression in prayer; and prayer is a dialogue. Revelation, too, that supernatural link which God has established with man, can likewise be looked upon as a dialogue."

By reaching out in dialogue to other Christians, and other religions, the Church is claiming and exploring its unique role in the world. I would say that we see this profile of the Church clearly embodied in the words and deeds of Pope Francis. That is why there has been such a strong response to him from people who are not Catholic, or not Christian or not religious. He is at the service of everyone and many people are touched and affirmed by him.

It is important to make the point that the dialogue agenda is not in any way in conflict with the Church's mission to evangelise. Dialogue and evangelisation are inextricably related. In a dialogue situation it is vital that the parties be able to articulate their faith clearly and robustly. It is equally vital that they be genuinely open and receptive to the testimony of their dialogue partners. Likewise, when we preach or teach the Gospel we create a dialogue situation in which an individual with his or her own story and experience engages with the Word of God.

The point has often been made that for there to be peace in the world, there must be peace between religions. For that reason and for many other reasons the re-publication of these texts is both timely and urgent. The documents are published here in the same form as they were originally published half a century ago.

Archbishop + Kevin McDonald

Director of the Office for Interreligious Relations and Chairman of the Committee for Catholic-Jewish Relations, Catholic Bishops' Conference of England and Wales.

Unitatis Redintegratio

- Decree on Ecumenism (1964)

UNITATIS REDINTEGRATIO
DECREE ON ECUMENISM

1. The restoration of unity among all Christians is one of the principal concerns of the Second Vatican Council. Christ the Lord founded one Church and one Church only. However, many Christian communions present themselves to men as the true inheritors of Jesus Christ; all indeed profess to be followers of the Lord but differ in mind and go their different ways, as if Christ Himself were divided.[1] Such division openly contradicts the will of Christ, scandalises the world, and damages the holy cause of preaching the Gospel to every creature.

But the Lord of Ages wisely and patiently follows out the plan of grace on our behalf, sinners that we are. In recent times more than ever before, He has been rousing divided Christians to remorse over their divisions and to a longing for unity. Everywhere large numbers have felt the impulse of this grace, and among our separated brethren also there increases from day to day the movement, fostered by the grace of the Holy Spirit, for the restoration of unity among all Christians. This movement toward unity is called "ecumenical". Those belong to it who invoke the Triune God and confess Jesus as Lord and Saviour, doing this not merely as individuals but also as corporate bodies. For almost everyone regards the body in which he has heard the Gospel as his Church and indeed, God's Church. All however, though in different ways, long for the one visible Church of God, a Church truly universal and set forth into the world that the world may be converted to the Gospel and so be saved, to the glory of God.

The Sacred Council gladly notes all this. It has already declared its teaching on the Church, and now, moved by a desire for the restoration of unity among all the followers of Christ, it wishes to set before all Catholics the ways and means by which they too can respond to this grace and to this divine call.

---

[1] Cf. *1 Co* 1:13.

CHAPTER I

CATHOLIC PRINCIPLES ON ECUMENISM

2. What has revealed the love of God among us is that the Father has sent into the world His only-begotten Son, so that, being made man, He might by His redemption give new life to the entire human race and unify it.[2] Before offering Himself up as a spotless victim upon the altar, Christ prayed to His Father for all who believe in Him: "that they all may be one; even as thou, Father, art in me, and I in thee, that they also may be one in us, so that the world may believe that thou has sent me".[3] In His Church He instituted the wonderful sacrament of the Eucharist by which the unity of His Church is both signified and made a reality. He gave His followers a new commandment to love one another,[4] and promised the Spirit, their Advocate,[5] who, as Lord and life-giver, should remain with them forever.

After being lifted up on the cross and glorified, the Lord Jesus poured forth His Spirit as He had promised, and through the Spirit He has called and gathered together the people of the New Covenant, who are the Church, into a unity of faith, hope and charity, as the Apostle teaches us: "There is one body and one Spirit, just as you were called to the one hope of your calling; one Lord, one faith, one Baptism".[6] For "all you who have been baptised into Christ have put on Christ...for you are all one in Christ Jesus".[7] It is the Holy Spirit, dwelling in those who believe and pervading and ruling over the Church as a whole, who brings about that wonderful communion of the faithful. He brings them

---

[2] Cf. *1 Jn* 4:9; *Col* 1:18-20; *Jn* 11:52.

[3] *Jn* 17:21.

[4] Cf. *Jn* 13:34.

[5] Cf. *Jn* 16:7.

[6] *Ep* 4:4-5.

[7] *Ga* 3:27-28.

into intimate union with Christ, so that He is the principle of the Church's unity. The distribution of graces and offices is His work too,[8] enriching the Church of Jesus Christ with different functions "in order to equip the saints for the work of service, so as to build up the body of Christ".[9]

In order to establish this His holy Church everywhere in the world till the end of time, Christ entrusted to the College of the Twelve the task of teaching, ruling and sanctifying.[10] Among their number He selected Peter, and after his confession of faith determined that on him He would build His Church. Also to Peter He promised the keys of the kingdom of heaven,[11] and after His profession of love, entrusted all His sheep to him to be confirmed in faith[12] and shepherded in perfect unity.[13] Christ Jesus Himself was forever to remain the chief cornerstone[14] and shepherd of our souls.[15]

Jesus Christ, then, willed that the apostles and their successors - the bishops with Peter's successor at their head - should preach the Gospel faithfully, administer the sacraments, and rule the Church in love. It is thus, under the action of the Holy Spirit, that Christ wills His people to increase, and He perfects His people's fellowship in unity: in their confessing the one faith, celebrating divine worship in common, and keeping the fraternal harmony of the family of God.

The Church, then, is God's only flock; it is like a standard lifted high for the nations to see it:[16] for it serves all mankind through the

---

[8] Cf. *1 Co* 12:4-11.

[9] *Ep* 4:12.

[10] Cf. *Mt* 28:18-20, *Jn* 20:21-23.

[11] Cf. *Mt* 16:18, *Mt* 18:18.

[12] Cf. *Lk* 22: 32.

[13] Cf. *Jn* 21:15-18.

[14] Cf. *Ep* 2:20.

[15] Cf. *1 Pt* 2:25; CONC. VATICANUM 1, Sess. IV (1870), *Constitutio Pastor Aeternus: Collac* 7, 482 a.

[16] Cf. *Is* 11:10-12.

Gospel of peace[17] as it makes its pilgrim way in hope toward the goal of the fatherland above.[18]

This is the sacred mystery of the unity of the Church, in Christ and through Christ, the Holy Spirit energising its various functions. It is a mystery that finds its highest exemplar and source in the unity of the Persons of the Trinity: the Father and the Son in the Holy Spirit, one God.

3. Even in the beginnings of this one and only Church of God there arose certain rifts,[19] which the Apostle strongly condemned.[20] But in subsequent centuries much more serious dissensions made their appearance and quite large communities came to be separated from full communion with the Catholic Church - for which, often enough, men of both sides were to blame. The children who are born into these Communities and who grow up believing in Christ cannot be accused of the sin involved in the separation, and the Catholic Church embraces upon them as brothers, with respect and affection. For men who believe in Christ and have been truly baptised are in communion with the Catholic Church even though this communion is imperfect. The differences that exist in varying degrees between them and the Catholic Church - whether in doctrine and sometimes in discipline, or concerning the structure of the Church - do indeed create many obstacles, sometimes serious ones, to full ecclesiastical communion. The ecumenical movement is striving to overcome these obstacles. But even in spite of them it remains true that all who have been justified by faith in Baptism are members of Christ's body,[21] and have a right to be called Christian, and so are correctly accepted as brothers by the children of the Catholic Church.[22]

---

[17] Cf. *Ep* 2:17-18, *Mk* 16:15.

[18] Cf. *1 Pt* 1:3-9.

[19] Cf. *1 Co* 11:18-19; *Gal* 1:6-9; *1 Jn* 2:18-19.

[20] Cf. *1 Co* 1:11; 11:22.

[21] Cf. CONC. FLORENTINUM, Sess. VIII (1439), *Decretum Exultate Deo:* Mansi 31, 1055. A.

[22] Cf. S. AUGUSTINUS, In *Ps*. 32, Enarr. 11, 29: PL 36, 299.

Moreover, some and even very many of the significant elements and endowments which together go to build up and give life to the Church itself, can exist outside the visible boundaries of the Catholic Church: the written word of God; the life of grace; faith, hope and charity, with the other interior gifts of the Holy Spirit, and visible elements too. All of these, which come from Christ and lead back to Christ, belong by right to the one Church of Christ.

The brethren divided from us also use many liturgical actions of the Christian religion. These most certainly can truly engender a life of grace in ways that vary according to the condition of each Church or Community. These liturgical actions must be regarded as capable of giving access to the community of salvation.

It follows that the separated Churches[23] and Communities as such, though we believe them to be deficient in some respects, have been by no means deprived of significance and importance in the mystery of salvation. For the Spirit of Christ has not refrained from using them as means of salvation which derive their efficacy from the very fullness of grace and truth entrusted to the Church.

Nevertheless, our separated brethren, whether considered as individuals or as Communities and Churches, are not blessed with that unity which Jesus Christ wished to bestow on all those who through Him were born again into one body, and with Him quickened to newness of life - that unity which the Holy Scriptures and the ancient Tradition of the Church proclaim. For it is only through Christ's Catholic Church, which is "the all-embracing means of salvation," that they can benefit fully from the means of salvation. We believe that Our Lord entrusted all the blessings of the New Covenant to the apostolic college alone, of which Peter is the head, in order to establish the one Body of Christ on earth to which all should be fully incorporated who belong in any way to the people of God. This people of God, though still in its members liable to sin, is ever growing in Christ during its pilgrimage on

---

[23] Cf. CONC. LATERANENSE IV (1215) *Constitutio IV*: Mansi 22, 990; CONC. LUGDUNENSE II (1274), *Professio fidei Michaelis Palaeologi*: Mansi 24, 71 E; CONC. FLORENTINUM, Sess. VI (1439), *Definitio Laetentur caeli*: Mansi 31, 1026 E.

earth, and is guided by God's gentle wisdom, according to His hidden designs, until it shall happily arrive at the fullness of eternal glory in the heavenly Jerusalem.

4. Today, in many parts of the world, under the inspiring grace of the Holy Spirit, many efforts are being made in prayer, word and action to attain that fullness of unity which Jesus Christ desires. The Sacred Council exhorts all the Catholic faithful to recognise the signs of the times and to take an active and intelligent part in the work of ecumenism.

The term "ecumenical movement" indicates the initiatives and activities planned and undertaken, according to the various needs of the Church and as opportunities offer, to promote Christian unity. These are: first, every effort to avoid expressions, judgements and actions which do not represent the condition of our separated brethren with truth and fairness and so make mutual relations with them more difficult; then, "dialogue" between competent experts from different Churches and Communities. At these meetings, which are organised in a religious spirit, each explains the teaching of his Communion in greater depth and brings out clearly its distinctive features. In such dialogue, everyone gains a truer knowledge and more just appreciation of the teaching and religious life of both Communions. In addition, the way is prepared for co-operation between them in the duties for the common good of humanity which are demanded by every Christian conscience; and, wherever this is allowed, there is prayer in common. Finally, all are led to examine their own faithfulness to Christ's will for the Church and accordingly to undertake with vigour the task of renewal and reform.

When such actions are undertaken prudently and patiently by the Catholic faithful, with the attentive guidance of their bishops, they promote justice and truth, concord and collaboration, as well as the spirit of brotherly love and unity. This is the way that, when the obstacles to perfect ecclesiastical communion have been gradually overcome, all Christians will at last, in a common celebration of the Eucharist, be gathered into the one and only Church in that unity which Christ bestowed on His Church from the beginning. We believe that this unity subsists in the Catholic Church as something she can never lose, and we hope that it will continue to increase until the end of time.

However, it is evident that, when individuals wish for full Catholic communion, their preparation and reconciliation is an undertaking which of its nature is distinct from ecumenical action. But there is no opposition between the two, since both proceed from the marvellous ways of God.

Catholics, in their ecumenical work, must assuredly be concerned for their separated brethren, praying for them, keeping them informed about the Church, making the first approaches toward them. But their primary duty is to make a careful and honest appraisal of whatever needs to be done or renewed in the Catholic household itself, in order that its life may bear witness more clearly and faithfully to the teachings and institutions which have come to it from Christ through the Apostles.

For although the Catholic Church has been endowed with all divinely revealed truth and with all means of grace, yet its members fail to live by them with all the fervour that they should, so that the radiance of the Church's image is less clear in the eyes of our separated brethren and of the world at large, and the growth of God's kingdom is delayed. All Catholics must therefore aim at Christian perfection[24] and, each according to his station, play his part that the Church may daily be more purified and renewed. For the Church must bear in her own body the humility and dying of Jesus,[25] against the day when Christ will present her to Himself in all her glory without spot or wrinkle.[26]

All in the Church must preserve unity in essentials. But let all, according to the gifts they have received enjoy a proper freedom, in their various forms of spiritual life and discipline, in their different liturgical rites, and even in their theological

---

[24] Cf. *Jm* 1:4; *Rm* 12:1-2.

[25] Cf. *2 Co* 4:10, *Ph* 2:5-8.

[26] Cf. *Ep* 5:27.

elaborations of revealed truth. In all things let charity prevail. If they are true to this course of action, they will be giving ever better expression to the authentic catholicity and apostolicity of the Church.

On the other hand, Catholics must gladly acknowledge and esteem the truly Christian endowments from our common heritage which are to be found among our separated brethren. It is right and salutary to recognise the riches of Christ and virtuous works in the lives of others who are bearing witness to Christ, sometimes even to the shedding of their blood. For God is always wonderful in His works and worthy of all praise.

Nor should we forget that anything wrought by the grace of the Holy Spirit in the hearts of our separated brethren can be a help to our own edification. Whatever is truly Christian is never contrary to what genuinely belongs to the faith; indeed, it can always bring a deeper realisation of the mystery of Christ and the Church.

Nevertheless, the divisions among Christians prevent the Church from attaining the fullness of catholicity proper to her, in those of her sons who, though attached to her by Baptism, are yet separated from full communion with her. Furthermore, the Church herself finds it more difficult to express in actual life her full catholicity in all her bearings.

This Sacred Council is gratified to note that the participation by the Catholic faithful in ecumenical work is growing daily. It commends this work to the bishops everywhere in the world to be vigorously stimulated by them and guided with prudence.

CHAPTER II

THE PRACTICE OF ECUMENISM

5. The attainment of union is the concern of the whole Church, faithful and shepherds alike. This concern extends to everyone, according to his talent, whether it be exercised in his daily Christian life or in his theological and historical research. This concern itself reveals already to some extent the bond of brotherhood between all Christians and it helps toward that full and perfect unity which God in His kindness wills.

6. Every renewal of the Church[27] is essentially grounded in an increase of fidelity to her own calling. Undoubtedly this is the basis of the movement toward unity.

Christ summons the Church to continual reformation as she sojourns here on earth. The Church is always in need of this, in so far as she is an institution of men here on earth. Thus if, in various times and circumstances, there have been deficiencies in moral conduct or in church discipline, or even in the way that church teaching has been formulated - to be carefully distinguished from the deposit of faith itself - these can and should be set right at the opportune moment.

Church renewal has therefore notable ecumenical importance. Already in various spheres of the Church's life, this renewal is taking place. The Biblical and liturgical movements, the preaching of the word of God and catechetics, the apostolate of the laity, new forms of religious life and the spirituality of married life, and the Church's social teaching and activity - all these should be considered as pledges and signs of the future progress of ecumenism.

7. There can be no ecumenism worthy of the name without a change of heart. For it is from renewal of the inner life of our minds,[28] from

---

[27] Cf. CONC. LATERANSE V, Sess. XII (1517), *Constitutio Constituti*: Mansi 32, 988 B-C.

[28] Cf. *Ep* 4:24.

self-denial and an unstinted love that desires of unity take their rise and develop in a mature way. We should therefore pray to the Holy Spirit for the grace to be genuinely self-denying, humble, gentle in the service of others, and to have an attitude of brotherly generosity towards them. St Paul says: "I, therefore, a prisoner for the Lord, beg you to lead a life worthy of the calling to which you have been called, with all humility and meekness, with patience, forbearing one another in love, eager to maintain the unity of the spirit in the bond of peace".[29] This exhortation is directed especially to those raised to sacred Orders precisely that the work of Christ may be continued. He came among us "not to be served but to serve".[30]

The words of St John hold good about sins against unity: "If we say we have not sinned, we make him a liar, and his word is not in us".[31] So we humbly beg pardon of God and of our separated brethren, just as we forgive them that trespass against us.

All the faithful should remember that the more effort they make to live holier lives according to the Gospel, the better will they further Christian unity and put it into practice. For the closer their union with the Father, the Word, and the Spirit, the more deeply and easily will they be able to grow in mutual brotherly love.

8. This change of heart and holiness of life, along with public and private prayer for the unity of Christians, should be regarded as the soul of the whole ecumenical movement, and merits the name, "spiritual ecumenism".

It is a recognised custom for Catholics to have frequent recourse to that prayer for the unity of the Church which the Saviour Himself on the eve of His death so fervently appealed to His Father: "That they may all be one".[32]

In certain special circumstances, such as the prescribed prayers "for unity," and during ecumenical gatherings, it is allowable,

---

[29] *Ep* 4:1-3.

[30] *Mt* 20:28.

[31] *1 Jn* 1:10.

[32] *Jn* 17:21.

indeed desirable that Catholics should join in prayer with their separated brethren. Such prayers in common are certainly an effective means of obtaining the grace of unity, and they are a true expression of the ties which still bind Catholics to their separated brethren. "For where two or three are gathered together in my name, there am I in the midst of them".[33]

Yet worship in common (*communicatio in sacris*) is not to be considered as a means to be used indiscriminately for the restoration of Christian unity. There are two main principles governing the practice of such common worship: first, the bearing witness to the unity of the Church, and second, the sharing in the means of grace. Witness to the unity of the Church very generally forbids common worship to Christians, but the grace to be had from it sometimes commends this practice. The course to be adopted, with due regard to all the circumstances of time, place, and persons, is to be decided by local episcopal authority, unless otherwise provided for by the Bishops' Conference according to its statutes, or by the Holy See.

9. We must get to know the outlook of our separated brethren. To achieve this purpose, study is of necessity required, and this must be pursued with a sense of realism and good will. Catholics, who already have a proper grounding, need to acquire a more adequate understanding of the respective doctrines of our separated brethren, their history, their spiritual and liturgical life, their religious psychology and general background. Most valuable for this purpose are meetings of the two sides - especially for discussion of theological problems - where each can deal with the other on an equal footing - provided that those who take part in them are truly competent and have the approval of the bishops. From such dialogue will emerge still more clearly what the situation of the Catholic Church really is. In this way too the outlook of our separated brethren will be better understood, and our own belief more aptly explained.

10. Sacred theology and other branches of knowledge, especially of a historical nature, must be taught with due regard for the

---

[33] *Mt* 18:20.

ecumenical point of view, so that they may correspond more exactly with the facts.

It is most important that future shepherds and priests should have mastered a theology that has been carefully worked out in this way and not polemically, especially with regard to those aspects which concern the relations of separated brethren with the Catholic Church.

This importance is the greater because the instruction and spiritual formation of the faithful and of religious depends so largely on the formation which their priests have received.

Moreover, Catholics engaged in missionary work in the same territories as other Christians ought to know, particularly in these times, the problems and the benefits in their apostolate which derive from the ecumenical movement.

11. The way and method in which the Catholic faith is expressed should never become an obstacle to dialogue with our brethren. It is, of course, essential that the doctrine should be clearly presented in its entirety. Nothing is so foreign to the spirit of ecumenism as a false irenicism, in which the purity of Catholic doctrine suffers loss and its genuine and certain meaning is clouded.

At the same time, the Catholic faith must be explained more profoundly and precisely, in such a way and in such terms as our separated brethren can also really understand.

Moreover, in ecumenical dialogue, Catholic theologians standing fast by the teaching of the Church and investigating the divine mysteries with the separated brethren must proceed with love for the truth, with charity, and with humility. When comparing doctrines with one another, they should remember that in Catholic doctrine there exists a "hierarchy" of truths, since they vary in their relation to the fundamental Christian faith. Thus the way will be opened by which through fraternal rivalry all will be stirred to a deeper understanding and a clearer presentation of the unfathomable riches of Christ.[34]

---

[34] Cf. *Ep* 3:8.

12. Before the whole world let all Christians confess their faith in the Triune God, one and three in the incarnate Son of God, our Redeemer and Lord. United in their efforts, and with mutual respect, let them bear witness to our common hope which does not play us false. In these days when co-operation in social matters is so widespread, all men without exception are called to work together, with much greater reason all those who believe in God, but most of all, all Christians in that they bear the name of Christ. Co-operation among Christians vividly expresses the relationship which in fact already unites them, and it sets in clearer relief the features of Christ the Servant. This co-operation, which has already begun in many countries, should be developed more and more, particularly in regions where a social and technical evolution is taking place be it in a just evaluation of the dignity of the human person, the establishment of the blessings of peace, the application of Gospel principles to social life, the advancement of the arts and sciences in a truly Christian spirit, or also in the use of various remedies to relieve the afflictions of our times such as famine and natural disasters, illiteracy and poverty, housing shortage and the unequal distribution of wealth. All believers in Christ can, through this co-operation, be led to acquire a better knowledge and appreciation of one another, and so pave the way to Christian unity.

CHAPTER III

CHURCHES AND ECCLESIAL COMMUNITIES SEPARATED FROM THE ROMAN APOSTOLIC SEE

13. We now turn our attention to the two chief types of division as they affect the seamless robe of Christ.

The first divisions occurred in the East, when the dogmatic formulae of the Councils of Ephesus and Chalcedon were challenged, and later when ecclesiastical communion between the Eastern Patriarchates and the Roman See was dissolved.

Other divisions arose more than four centuries later in the West, stemming from the events which are usually referred to as "The Reformation". As a result, many Communions, national or confessional, were separated from the Roman See. Among those in which Catholic traditions and institutions in part continue to exist, the Anglican Communion occupies a special place.

These various divisions differ greatly from one another not only by reason of their origin, place and time, but especially in the nature and seriousness of questions bearing on faith and the structure of the Church. Therefore, without minimizing the differences between the various Christian bodies, and without overlooking the bonds between them which exist in spite of divisions, this holy Council decides to propose the following considerations for prudent ecumenical action.

I. The Special Consideration of the Eastern Churches

14. For many centuries the Church of the East and that of the West each followed their separate ways though linked in a brotherly union of faith and sacramental life; the Roman See by common consent acted as guide when disagreements arose between them over matters of faith or discipline. Among other matters of great importance, it is a pleasure for this Council to remind everyone that

there flourish in the East many particular or local Churches, among which the Patriarchal Churches hold first place, and of these not a few pride themselves in tracing their origins back to the apostles themselves. Hence a matter of primary concern and care among the Easterns, in their local churches, has been, and still is, to preserve the family ties of common faith and charity which ought to exist between sister Churches.

Similarly it must not be forgotten that from the beginning the Churches of the East have had a treasury from which the Western Church has drawn extensively - in liturgical practice, spiritual tradition, and law. Nor must we undervalue the fact that it was the ecumenical councils held in the East that defined the basic dogmas of the Christian faith, on the Trinity, on the Word of God Who took flesh of the Virgin Mary. To preserve this faith these Churches have suffered and still suffer much.

However, the heritage handed down by the apostles was received with differences of form and manner, so that from the earliest times of the Church it was explained variously in different places, owing to diversities of genius and conditions of life. All this, quite apart from external causes, prepared the way for decisions arising also from a lack of charity and mutual understanding.

For this reason the Holy Council urges all, but especially those who intend to devote themselves to the restoration of full communion hoped for between the Churches of the East and the Catholic Church, to give due consideration to this special feature of the origin and growth of the Eastern Churches, and to the character of the relations which obtained between them and the Roman See before separation. They must take full account of all these factors and, where this is done, it will greatly contribute to the dialogue that is looked for.

15. Everyone also knows with what great love the Christians of the East celebrate the sacred liturgy, especially the Eucharistic celebration, source of the Church's life and pledge of future glory, in which the faithful, united with their bishop, have access to God the Father through the Son, the Word made flesh, Who suffered

and has been glorified, and so, in the outpouring of the Holy Spirit, they enter into communion with the most holy Trinity, being made "sharers of the divine nature".[35] Hence, through the celebration of the Holy Eucharist in each of these churches, the Church of God is built up and grows in stature[36] and through concelebration, their communion with one another is made manifest.

In this liturgical worship, the Christians of the East pay high tribute, in beautiful hymns of praise, to Mary ever Virgin, whom the ecumenical Council of Ephesus solemnly proclaimed to be the holy Mother of God, so that Christ might be acknowledged as being truly Son of God and Son of Man, according to the Scriptures. Many also are the saints whose praise they sing, among them the Fathers of the universal Church.

These Churches, although separated from us, possess true sacraments, above all by apostolic succession, the priesthood and the Eucharist, whereby they are linked with us in closest intimacy. Therefore some worship in common (*communicatio in sacris*), given suitable circumstances and the approval of Church authority, is not only possible but to be encouraged.

Moreover, in the East are found the riches of those spiritual traditions which are given expression especially in monastic life. There from the glorious times of the holy Fathers, monastic spirituality flourished which, then later flowed over into the Western world, and there provided the source from which Latin monastic life took its rise and has drawn fresh vigour ever since. Catholics therefore are earnestly recommended to avail themselves of the spiritual riches of the Eastern Fathers which lift up the whole man to the contemplation of the divine.

The very rich liturgical and spiritual heritage of the Eastern Churches should be known, venerated, preserved and cherished by all. They must recognise that this is of supreme importance for the faithful preservation of the fullness of Christian tradition, and

---

[35] 2 *Pt* 1:4.
[36] Cf. S. IOANNES CHRYSOSTOMOS, *In Ioannem Homelia XLVI*, PG 59, 260-262.

for bringing about reconciliation between Eastern and Western Christians.

16. Already from the earliest times the Eastern Churches followed their own forms of ecclesiastical law and custom, which were sanctioned by the approval of the Fathers of the Church, of synods, and even of ecumenical councils. Far from being an obstacle to the Church's unity, a certain diversity of customs and observances only adds to her splendor, and is of great help in carrying out her mission, as has already been stated. To remove, then, all shadow of doubt, this holy Council solemnly declares that the Churches of the East, while remembering the necessary unity of the whole Church, have the power to govern themselves according to the disciplines proper to them, since these are better suited to the character of their faithful, and more for the good of their souls. The perfect observance of this traditional principle not always indeed carried out in practice, is one of the essential prerequisites for any restoration of unity.

17. What has just been said about the lawful variety that can exist in the Church must also be taken to apply to the differences in theological expression of doctrine. In the study of revelation East and West have followed different methods, and have developed differently their understanding and confession of God's truth. It is hardly surprising, then, if from time to time one tradition has come nearer to a full appreciation of some aspects of a mystery of revelation than the other, or has expressed it to better advantage. In such cases, these various theological expressions are to be considered often as mutually complementary rather than conflicting. Where the authentic theological traditions of the Eastern Church are concerned, we must recognise the admirable way in which they have their roots in Holy Scripture, and how they are nurtured and given expression in the life of the liturgy. They derive their strength too from the living tradition of the apostles and from the works of the Fathers and spiritual writers of the Eastern Churches. Thus they promote the right ordering of Christian life and, indeed, pave the way to a full vision of Christian truth.

All this heritage of spirituality and liturgy, of discipline and theology, in its various traditions, this holy synod declares to belong to the full Catholic and apostolic character of the Church. We thank God that many Eastern children of the Catholic Church, who preserve this heritage, and wish to express it more faithfully and completely in their lives, are already living in full communion with their brethren who follow the tradition of the West.

18. After taking all these factors into consideration, this Sacred Council solemnly repeats the declaration of previous Councils and Roman Pontiffs, that for the restoration or the maintenance of unity and communion it is necessary "to impose no burden beyond what is essential".[37] It is the Council's urgent desire that, in the various organisations and living activities of the Church, every effort should be made toward the gradual realisation of this unity, especially by prayer, and by fraternal dialogue on points of doctrine and the more pressing pastoral problems of our time. Similarly, the Council commends to the shepherds and faithful of the Catholic Church to develop closer relations with those who are no longer living in the East but are far from home, so that friendly collaboration with them may increase, in the spirit of love, to the exclusion of all feeling of rivalry or strife. If this cause is wholeheartedly promoted, the Council hopes that the barrier dividing the Eastern Church and Western Church will be removed, and that at last there may be but the one dwelling, firmly established on Christ Jesus, the cornerstone, who will make both one.[38]

II. Separated Churches and Ecclesial Communities in the West

19. In the great upheaval which began in the West toward the end of the Middle Ages, and in later times too, Churches and ecclesial Communities came to be separated from the Apostolic See of Rome. Yet they have retained a particularly close affinity with

---

[37] *Ac* 15:28.
[38] Cf. CONC. FLORENTINUM, Sess. VI (1439), *Definitio Laetentur caeli*: Mansi 31 1026 E.

the Catholic Church as a result of the long centuries in which all Christendom lived together in ecclesiastical communion.

However, since these Churches and ecclesial Communities, on account of their different origins, and different teachings in matters of doctrine on the spiritual life, vary considerably not only with us, but also among themselves, the task of describing them at all adequately is extremely difficult; and we have no intention of making such an attempt here.

Although the ecumenical movement and the desire for peace with the Catholic Church have not yet taken hold everywhere, it is our hope that ecumenical feeling and mutual esteem may gradually increase among all men.

It must however be admitted that in these Churches and ecclesial Communities there exist important differences from the Catholic Church, not only of a historical, sociological, psychological and cultural character, but especially in the interpretation of revealed truth. To make easier the ecumenical dialogue in spite of these differences, we wish to set down some considerations which can, and indeed should, serve as a basis and encouragement for such dialogue.

20. Our thoughts turn first to those Christians who make open confession of Jesus Christ as God and Lord and as the sole Mediator between God and men, to the glory of the one God, Father, Son and Holy Spirit. We are aware indeed that there exist considerable divergences from the doctrine of the Catholic Church concerning Christ Himself, the Word of God made flesh, the work of redemption, and consequently, concerning the mystery and ministry of the Church, and the role of Mary in the plan of salvation. But we rejoice to see that our separated brethren look to Christ as the source and centre of Church unity. Their longing for union with Christ inspires them to seek an ever closer unity, and also to bear witness to their faith among the peoples of the earth.

21. A love and reverence of Sacred Scripture which might be described as devotion, leads our brethren to a constant meditative study of the sacred text. For the Gospel "is the power of God for salvation to everyone who has faith, to the Jew first and then to the Greek".[39]

While invoking the Holy Spirit, they seek in these very Scriptures God as it were speaking to them in Christ, Whom the prophets foretold, Who is the Word of God made flesh for us. They contemplate in the Scriptures the life of Christ and what the Divine Master taught and did for our salvation, especially the mysteries of His death and resurrection.

But while the Christians who are separated from us hold the divine authority of the Sacred Books, they differ from ours - some in one way, some in another - regarding the relationship between Scripture and the Church. For, according to Catholic belief, the authentic teaching authority of the Church has a special place in the interpretation and preaching of the written word of God.

But Sacred Scriptures provide for the work of dialogue an instrument of the highest value in the mighty hand of God for the attainment of that unity which the Saviour holds out to all.

22. Whenever the Sacrament of Baptism is duly administered as Our Lord instituted it, and is received with the right dispositions, a person is truly incorporated into the crucified and glorified Christ, and reborn to a sharing of the divine life, as the Apostle says: "You were buried together with Him in Baptism, and in Him also rose again - through faith in the working of God, who raised Him from the dead".[40]

Baptism therefore establishes a sacramental bond of unity which links all who have been reborn by it. But of itself Baptism is only a beginning, an inauguration wholly directed toward the fullness of life in Christ. Baptism, therefore, envisages a complete profession of faith, complete incorporation in the system of salvation such as

---

[39] *Rm* 1:16.
[40] *Col* 2:12; cf. *Rm* 6:4.

Christ willed it to be, and finally complete ingrafting in eucharistic communion.

Though the ecclesial Communities which are separated from us lack the fullness of unity with us flowing from Baptism, and though we believe they have not retained the proper reality of the eucharistic mystery in its fullness, especially because of the absence of the Sacrament of Orders, nevertheless when they commemorate His death and resurrection in the Lord's Supper, they profess that it signifies life in communion with Christ and look forward to His coming in glory. Therefore the teaching concerning the Lord's Supper, the other sacraments, worship, the ministry of the Church, must be the subject of the dialogue.

23. The daily Christian life of these brethren is nourished by their faith in Christ and strengthened by the grace of Baptism and by hearing the word of God. This shows itself in their private prayer, their meditation on the Bible, in their Christian family life, and in the worship of a community gathered together to praise God. Moreover, their form of worship sometimes displays notable features of the liturgy which they shared with us of old.

Their faith in Christ bears fruit in praise and thanksgiving for the blessings received from the hands of God. Among them, too, is a strong sense of justice and a true charity toward their neighbour. This active faith has been responsible for many organisations for the relief of spiritual and material distress, the furtherance of the education of youth, the improvement of the social conditions of life, and the promotion of peace throughout the world.

While it is true that many Christians understand the moral teaching of the Gospel differently from Catholics, and do not accept the same solutions to the more difficult problems of modern society, nevertheless they share our desire to stand by the words of Christ as the source of Christian virtue, and to obey the command of the Apostle: "And whatever you do, in word or in work, do all in the name of the Lord Jesus Christ, giving thanks to God the Father through Him".[41] For that reason an ecumenical dialogue

---

[41] *Col* 3:17.

might start with discussion of the application of the Gospel to moral conduct.

24. Now that we have briefly set out the conditions for ecumenical action and the principles by which it is to be directed, we look with confidence to the future. This Sacred Council exhorts the faithful to refrain from superficiality and imprudent zeal, which can hinder real progress toward unity. Their ecumenical action must be fully and sincerely Catholic, that is to say, faithful to the truth which we have received from the apostles and Fathers of the Church, in harmony with the faith which the Catholic Church has always professed, and at the same time directed toward that fullness to which Our Lord wills His Body to grow in the course of time.

It is the urgent wish of this Holy Council that the measures undertaken by the sons of the Catholic Church should develop in conjunction with those of our separated brethren so that no obstacle be put in the ways of divine Providence and no preconceived judgements impair the future inspirations of the Holy Spirit. The Council moreover professes its awareness that human powers and capacities cannot achieve this holy objective - the reconciling of all Christians in the unity of the one and only Church of Christ. It is because of this that the Council rests all its hope on the prayer of Christ for the Church, on our Father's love for us, and on the power of the Holy Spirit". "And hope does not disappoint, because God's love has been poured into our hearts through the Holy Spirit, who has been given to us".[42]

Each and all these matters which are set forth in this Decree have been favourably voted on by the Fathers of the Council. And We, by the apostolic authority given Us by Christ and in union with the Fathers, approve, decree and establish them in the Holy Spirit and command that they be promulgated for the glory of God.

Given in Rome at St Peter's, 21st November, 1964

---

[42] *Rm* 5:5.

Nostra Aetate

- Declaration on the Relation of the Church to Non-Christian Religions (1965)

NOSTRA AETATE DECLARATION ON THE RELATION OF THE CHURCH TO NON-CHRISTIAN RELIGIONS

PROCLAIMED BY HIS HOLINESS POPE PAUL VI ON 28TH OCTOBER, 1965

1. In our time, when day by day mankind is being drawn closer together, and the ties between different peoples are becoming stronger, the Church examines more closely her relationship to non-Christian religions. In her task of promoting unity and love among men, indeed among nations, she considers above all in this declaration what men have in common and what draws them to fellowship.

One is the community of all peoples, one their origin, for God made the whole human race to live over the face of the earth.[1] One also is their final goal, God. His providence, His manifestations of goodness, His saving design extend to all men,[2] until that time when the elect will be united in the Holy City, the city ablaze with the glory of God, where the nations will walk in His light.[3]

Men expect from the various religions answers to the unsolved riddles of the human condition, which today, even as in former times, deeply stir the hearts of men: What is man? What is the meaning, the aim of our life? What is moral good, what is sin? Whence suffering and what purpose does it serve? Which is the road to true happiness? What are death, judgement and retribution after death? What, finally, is that ultimate inexpressible mystery which encompasses our existence: whence do we come, and where are we going?

---

[1] Cf. *Ac* 17:26.

[2] Cf. *Ws* 8:1; *Ac* 14:17; *Rm* 2:6-7; *1 Tm.* 2:4.

[3] Cf. *Rv* 21:23f.

2. From ancient times down to the present, there is found among various peoples a certain perception of that hidden power which hovers over the course of things and over the events of human history; at times some indeed have come to the recognition of a Supreme Being, or even of a Father. This perception and recognition penetrates their lives with a profound religious sense.

Religions, however, that are bound up with an advanced culture have struggled to answer the same questions by means of more refined concepts and a more developed language. Thus in Hinduism, men contemplate the divine mystery and express it through an inexhaustible abundance of myths and through searching philosophical inquiry. They seek freedom from the anguish of our human condition either through ascetical practices or profound meditation or a flight to God with love and trust. Again, Buddhism, in its various forms, realises the radical insufficiency of this changeable world; it teaches a way by which men, in a devout and confident spirit, may be able either to acquire the state of perfect liberation, or attain, by their own efforts or through higher help, supreme illumination. Likewise, other religions found everywhere try to counter the restlessness of the human heart, each in its own manner, by proposing "ways", comprising teachings, rules of life, and sacred rites. The Catholic Church rejects nothing that is true and holy in these religions. She regards with sincere reverence those ways of conduct and of life, those precepts and teachings which, though differing in many aspects from the ones she holds and sets forth, nonetheless often reflect a ray of that Truth which enlightens all men. Indeed, she proclaims, and ever must proclaim Christ "the way, the truth, and the life" (*Jn* 14:6), in whom men may find the fullness of religious life, in whom God has reconciled all things to Himself.[4]

The Church, therefore, exhorts her sons, that through dialogue and collaboration with the followers of other religions, carried out with prudence and love and in witness to the Christian faith and life, they recognise, preserve and promote the good things, spiritual and moral, as well as the socio-cultural values found among these men.

---

[4] Cf 2 *Co* 5:18-19.

3. The Church regards with esteem also the Moslems. They adore the one God, living and subsisting in Himself; merciful and all-powerful, the Creator of heaven and earth,[5] who has spoken to men; they take pains to submit wholeheartedly to even His inscrutable decrees, just as Abraham, with whom the faith of Islam takes pleasure in linking itself, submitted to God. Though they do not acknowledge Jesus as God, they revere Him as a prophet. They also honour Mary, His virgin Mother; at times they even call on her with devotion. In addition, they await the day of judgement when God will render their deserts to all those who have been raised up from the dead. Finally, they value the moral life and worship God especially through prayer, almsgiving and fasting.

Since in the course of centuries not a few quarrels and hostilities have arisen between Christians and Moslems, this sacred synod urges all to forget the past and to work sincerely for mutual understanding and to preserve as well as to promote together for the benefit of all mankind social justice and moral welfare, as well as peace and freedom.

4. As the sacred synod searches into the mystery of the Church, it remembers the bond that spiritually ties the people of the New Covenant to Abraham's stock.

Thus the Church of Christ acknowledges that, according to God's saving design, the beginnings of her faith and her election are found already among the Patriarchs, Moses and the prophets. She professes that all who believe in Christ - Abraham's sons according to faith[6] - are included in the same Patriarch's call, and likewise that the salvation of the Church is mysteriously foreshadowed by the chosen people's exodus from the land of bondage. The Church, therefore, cannot forget that she received the revelation of the Old Testament through the people with whom God in His inexpressible mercy concluded the Ancient Covenant. Nor can she forget that she draws sustenance from the root of that

---

[5] Cf St Gregory VII, Letter XXI to *Anzir (Nacir), King of Mauritania* (Pl. 148, col. 450f).

[6] Cf. *Ga* 3:7.

well-cultivated olive tree onto which have been grafted the wild shoots, the Gentiles.[7] Indeed, the Church believes that by His cross Christ, Our Peace, reconciled Jews and Gentiles, making both one in Himself.[8]

The Church keeps ever in mind the words of the Apostle about his kinsmen: "theirs is the sonship and the glory and the covenants and the law and the worship and the promises; theirs are the fathers and from them is the Christ according to the flesh" (*Rm* 9:4-5), the Son of the Virgin Mary. She also recalls that the Apostles, the Church's main-stay and pillars, as well as most of the early disciples who proclaimed Christ's Gospel to the world, sprang from the Jewish people.

As Holy Scripture testifies, Jerusalem did not recognise the time of her visitation,[9] nor did the Jews in large number, accept the Gospel; indeed not a few opposed its spreading.[10] Nevertheless, God holds the Jews most dear for the sake of their Fathers; He does not repent of the gifts He makes or of the calls He issues - such is the witness of the Apostle.[11] In company with the prophets and the same Apostle, the Church awaits that day, known to God alone, on which all peoples will address the Lord in a single voice and "serve him shoulder to shoulder" (*Zp* 3:9).[12]

Since the spiritual patrimony common to Christians and Jews is thus so great, this sacred synod wants to foster and recommend that mutual understanding and respect which is the fruit, above all, of biblical and theological studies as well as of fraternal dialogues.

True, the Jewish authorities and those who followed their lead pressed for the death of Christ;[13] still, what happened in

---

[7] Cf. *Rm* 11:17-24.

[8] Cf. *Ep* 2:14-16.

[9] Cf. *Lk* 19:44.

[10] Cf. *Rm* 11:28.

[11] Cf. *Rm* 11:28-29; cf. dogmatic Constitution, *Lumen Gentium* (Light of nations) AAS, 57 (1965) p. 20.

[12] Cf. *Is* 66:23; *Ps* 65:4; *Rm* 11:11-32.

[13] Cf. *Jn* 19:6.

His passion cannot be charged against all the Jews, without distinction, then alive, nor against the Jews of today. Although the Church is the new people of God, the Jews should not be presented as rejected or accursed by God, as if this followed from the Holy Scriptures. All should see to it, then, that in catechetical work or in the preaching of the word of God they do not teach anything that does not conform to the truth of the Gospel and the spirit of Christ.

Furthermore, in her rejection of every persecution against any man, the Church, mindful of the patrimony she shares with the Jews and moved not by political reasons but by the Gospel's spiritual love, decries hatred, persecutions, displays of anti-Semitism, directed against Jews at any time and by anyone.

Besides, as the Church has always held and holds now, Christ underwent His passion and death freely, because of the sins of men and out of infinite love, in order that all may reach salvation. It is, therefore, the burden of the Church's preaching to proclaim the cross of Christ as the sign of God's all-embracing love and as the fountain from which every grace flows.

5. We cannot truly call on God, the Father of all, if we refuse to treat in a brotherly way any man, created as he is in the image of God. Man's relation to God the Father and his relation to men his brothers are so linked together that Scripture says: "He who does not love does not know God" (*1 Jn* 4:8).

No foundation therefore remains for any theory or practice that leads to discrimination between man and man or people and people, so far as their human dignity and the rights flowing from it are concerned.

The Church reproves, as foreign to the mind of Christ, any discrimination against men or harassment of them because of their race, colour, condition of life, or religion. On the contrary, following in the footsteps of the holy Apostles Peter and Paul, this sacred synod ardently implores the Christian faithful to "maintain good fellowship among the nations" (*1 Pt* 2:12), and, if possible, to live for their part in peace with all men,[14] so that they may truly be sons of the Father who is in heaven.[15]

[14] Cf. *Rm* 12:18.
[15] Cf. *Mt* 5:45.

Ecclesiam Suam

- Encyclical of Pope Paul VI on the Church (1964)

ECCLESIAM SUAM
ENCYCLICAL OF POPE PAUL VI
ON THE CHURCH 6TH AUGUST, 1964

To His Venerable Brethren the Patriarchs, Primates, Archbishops, Bishops, and other Local Ordinaries who are at Peace and Communion with the Apostolic See, to the Clergy and faithful of the entire world, and to all men of good will.

Venerable Brethren and Dearest Sons Health and Apostolic Benediction.

1. The Church was founded by Jesus Christ to be the loving mother of the whole human family and minister to its salvation. All through the centuries, therefore, whenever men have yearned for the glory of Almighty God and the eternal salvation of souls, they have naturally made the Church the special object of their devotion and concern. We find, of course, outstanding examples of such men in the persons of Christ's vicars on earth, countless thousands of bishops and priests, and a wonderful host of saintly Christians.

2. It will not, therefore, come as a surprise when We acknowledge that Our own thoughts as We sit down to write this first encyclical of Our sovereign pontificate - to which God in his inscrutable designs has called Us - are naturally and inevitably concerned with the loving and reverent consideration of the subject of Holy Church.

What the Encyclical Intends

3. The aim of this encyclical will be to demonstrate with increasing clarity how vital it is for the world, and how greatly desired by the Catholic Church, that the two should meet together, and get to know and love one another.

4. Last year We were given by God's merciful grace a golden opportunity of addressing you in person. It was on the feast of the Archangel Michael, when you were assembled together in St Peter's basilica for the opening of the second session of Vatican II. We told you on that occasion that it was Our intention to do what other popes have done on their accession to the pontifical office: to write to you as your Father and Brother an encyclical letter proclaiming the policies which are uppermost in Our thoughts and which seem to Us to have a considerable practical bearing on the conduct of the first years of Our pontificate.

5. The declaration of these policies is not, in fact, an easy matter. All such policies must be derived first of all from an earnest consideration of divine doctrine, for even Christ Himself, we must remember, said: "My doctrine is not mine, but his who sent me."[1] Then they must be shown to measure up to the present state of the Church, a state in which the Church's interior life is still vigorous, having stood the test of long experience, and its exterior energies are powerfully directed toward the work of the apostolate. And finally We must bear in mind the actual situation in which human society today finds itself. Our task is to serve society.

What It Does Not Intend

6. But Our present aim is not to expound new or duly developed insights. That is the proper task of the Ecumenical Council. It is certainly not Our wish to disrupt the work of the council in this simple, conversational letter of Ours, but rather to commend it and to stimulate it.

7. Nor do We propose to make this encyclical a solemn proclamation of Catholic doctrine or of moral or social principles. Our purpose is merely to send you a sincere message, as between brothers and members of a common family. We do so in fulfilment of Our duty and with no other thought in mind than to open Our heart to you and to strengthen more and more and render more joyful that

---

[1] *Jn* 7:16.

union of faith and love which happily exists between us. We aim at increasingly better results from our pastoral activity, a more fruitful outcome of the sessions of the Ecumenical Council, and a clearer exposition of those doctrinal and practical rules which govern the spiritual and apostolic activity of the official rulers of the Church, their subjects, collaborators and well-wishers.

THREE PRINCIPAL POLICIES
OF THE PONTIFICATE

8. In short, Venerable Brethren, there are three policies which principally exercise Our mind when We reflect on the enormous responsibility for the Church of Christ which, unsought and undeserved, the providence of God has laid upon Us in making Us Bishop of Rome, successor to St Peter the Apostle and Key-bearer of the Kingdom of Heaven, and Vicar of Christ who appointed Peter the first Shepherd of his worldwide flock.

Deeper Self-Knowledge Essential

9. First We are convinced that the Church must look with penetrating eyes within itself, ponder the mystery of its own being, and draw enlightenment and inspiration from a deeper scrutiny of the doctrine of its own origin, nature, mission, and destiny. The doctrine is already known; it has been developed and popularised in the course of this century. But it can never claim to be sufficiently investigated and understood, for it contains "the publication of a mystery, kept hidden from the beginning of time in the all-creating mind of God...in order that it may be known...through the Church."[2] It is a storehouse of God's hidden counsels which the Church must bring to light. It is a doctrine which more than any other is arousing the expectation and attention of every faithful follower of Christ, and especially of men like us, Venerable Brethren, whom "the Holy Spirit has appointed to rule the very Church of God."[3]

10. A vivid and lively self-awareness on the part of the Church inevitably leads to a comparison between the ideal image of the Church as Christ envisaged it, His holy and spotless bride,[4] and the actual image which the Church presents to the world today. This actual image does indeed, thank God, truly bear those characteristics

[2] Cf. *Ep* 3:9-10.
[3] Cf. *Ac* 20:28.
[4] Cf. *Ep* 5:27.

impressed on it by its divine Founder; and in the course of the centuries the Holy Spirit has accentuated and enhanced these traits so as to make the Church conform more and more to the original intention of its Founder and to the particular genius of human society which it is continually striving to win over to itself through the preaching of the gospel of salvation. But the actual image of the Church will never attain to such a degree of perfection, beauty, holiness and splendour that it can be said to correspond perfectly with the original conception in the mind of Him who fashioned it.

Renewal the inevitable result

11. Hence the Church's heroic and impatient struggle for renewal: the struggle to correct those flaws introduced by its members which its own self-examination, mirroring its exemplar, Christ, points out to it and condemns. And this brings us, Venerable Brethren, to the second policy We have in mind at this time: to bring the members of the Church to a clearer realisation of their duty to correct their faults, strive for perfection, and make a wise choice of the means necessary for achieving the renewal We spoke of. We tell you this not only that We may Ourself find greater courage to introduce the appropriate reforms, but also in order to secure your sympathy, advice, and support in a matter of such urgency and difficulty.

Dialogue to be extended

12. These two policies of Ours-which are yours, of course, as well-lead naturally to a third policy, which has to do with the relations which the Church must establish with the surrounding world in which it lives and works.

13. One part of this world, as everyone knows, has in recent years detached itself and broken away from the Christian foundations of its culture, although formerly it had been so imbued with Christianity and had drawn from it such strength and vigour that the people of these nations in many cases owe to Christianity all

that is best in their own tradition - a fact that is not always fully appreciated. Another and larger part of the world covers the vast territories of the so-called emerging nations. Taken as a whole, it is a world which offers to the Church not one but a hundred forms of possible contacts, some of which are open and easy, others difficult and problematic, and many, unfortunately, wholly unfavourable to friendly dialogue.

14. It is at this point, therefore, that the problem of the Church's dialogue with the modern world arises. It will be for the Council to determine the extent and complexity of this problem and to do what it can to devise suitable methods for its solution. But the very need to solve it is felt by Us - and by you too, whose experience of the urgency of the problem is no less than Our own - as a responsibility, a stimulus, an inner urge about which We cannot remain silent. We have thought fit to put this important and complex matter before you in council, and we must do what we can to make ourselves better prepared for these discussions and deliberations.

15. It will, of course, be clear to you from this brief outline of the contents of this encyclical that We have no intention of dealing here with all the serious and pressing problems affecting humanity no less than the Church at this present time; such questions as peace among nations and among social classes, the destitution and famine which still plague entire populations, the advance of the new nations toward independence and civilisation, the current of modern thought over against Christian culture, the difficulties experienced by so many nations and by the Church in those extensive parts of the world where the rights of free citizens and of human beings are being denied, the moral problems concerning the population explosion, and so on.

Peace: A Matter of Special Urgency

16. What we cannot, however, fail to mention here is the fact that We are acutely conscious of Our duty to pay particular attention to the serious problem of world peace. It is a problem which demands Our

48

continuous personal involvement and practical concern, exercised of course within the limits of Our own ministry and entirely divorced from any set political theory and from considerations of Our own personal and purely temporal advantage. Our aim must be to educate mankind to sentiments and policies which are opposed to violent and deadly conflicts and to foster just, rational, and peaceful relations between States. We will do Our utmost to promote harmonious relations and a spirit of co-operation between nations, and We will do so by proclaiming principles which represent the highest achievement of human thought, and such as are best calculated to allay the selfishness and greed from which war takes its rise. Nor, if We are allowed the opportunity, will We fail to use our good offices in settling national disputes on a basis of fraternity and honour. We do not forget that this service, besides being one dictated by love, is in fact a plain duty. It is a duty which the awareness of Our mission in the modern world renders all the more imperative when we consider the advances that have been made in theology and in international institutions. Our mission is to bring men together in mutual love through the power of that kingdom of justice and peace which Christ inaugurated by His coming into the world.

17. If, therefore, We confine Ourself here to a logical and fact-finding disquisition on the life of the Church, this does not mean that We are dismissing from Our mind those other highly important issues. Some of them will be coming up before the Council for consideration, and We too, during the course of Our apostolic ministry, will study them and endeavour to a practical solution to them, God giving Us the inspiration and the strength.

I. SELF-AWARENESS

18. We believe that it is a duty of the Church at the present time to strive toward a clearer and deeper awareness of itself and its mission in the world, and of the treasury of truth of which it is heir and custodian. Thus before embarking on the study of any particular problem and before considering what attitude to adopt vis-a-vis the world, the Church must here and now reflect on its own nature, the better to appreciate the divine plan which it is the Church's task to implement. By doing this it will find a more revealing light, new energy and increased joy in the fulfilment of its own mission, and discover better ways of augmenting the effectiveness and fruitfulness of its contacts with the world. For the Church does indeed belong to the world, even though distinguished from it by its own altogether unique characteristics.

THE ACT OF FAITH

19. This act of self-examination on the part of the Church seems to Us to accord well with the method employed by God in revealing himself to men and initiating that religious, two-way relationship between God and man which is what the Church both effects in the world and manifests in itself. For whereas it is true that divine revelation was made "in divers ways and at divers times,"[5] in an incontestably historical setting, it is also true that it was able to effect an entry into the very life of men by means involving both human speech and divine grace. Grace comes secretly into the soul after the hearing of the message of salvation. This is followed by the act of faith, the beginning of our justification.

20. We would wish this reflection on the origin and nature of those new and vital relationships which the Christian religion establishes between God and man to assume the character of an act of willing submission to what the divine Teacher said to those who listened to Him, and especially to the disciples, among whom we today rightly

---

[5] *Heb* 1:1.

rejoice to be numbered. From the many insistent and frequently reiterated commands of Our Lord We select one which would seem to have special relevance for Christ's faithful followers at the present time, namely that concerning Christian vigilance.

Christ's Exhortation to Vigilance

21. Now it is true that our Master's warning in this respect referred primarily to the need to be on the watch for the end of the world, which will have to come sooner or later. But precisely because this vigilance must always be present and operative in the mind of the faithful servant, it follows that everything that he sets his hand to, his whole way of life as a Christian in the world, should conform to this rule.

Our Lord's exhortation to vigilance is equally applicable to things which may be of more immediate concern to us, the dangers and temptations which threaten to corrupt men's moral lives and turn men away from the right path of truth.[6] Thus it is easy to discover in the Gospel a continuous appeal to right thought and action. Was this not in fact the theme of Our Lord's forerunner, St John, whose preaching inaugurates in the Gospel the public ministry of Jesus Christ? And did not Jesus Christ Himself call upon men to receive God's kingdom interiorly?[7] Was not His whole teaching technique concerned with inculcating and fostering the soul's interior life? As a necessary condition for receiving the supernatural gifts of truth and grace in a way consistent with the dignity of the human person, Christ aimed at developing in men a psychological as well as a moral awareness. This awareness was an awareness of their discipleship, which was later to have the effect of recalling to their minds everything that Jesus had taught them and everything that had happened to Him.[8] It would grow to maturity, and then at last men would understand who Jesus was, and the meaning of what He had taught and done.

---

[6] Cf. *Mt* 26:41.

[7] Cf. *Lk* 17:21.

[8] Cf. *Mt* 26:75; *Lk* 24:8; *Jn* 14:26; 16:4.

22. The Church's awareness of its divine mission coincided with its birth. Both events are celebrated at Pentecost. Both will develop together. The Church, that is, will develop as a well-organised, hierarchic and social body, and at the same time its awareness of its vocation, of its inner nature, its doctrine, and its mission, will likewise develop. That is what St Paul prayed for when he said: "And this I pray, that your charity may more and more abound in knowledge and in all understanding."[9]

Renewed Profession of Faith

23. In other words, Venerable Brethren, We are exhorting everyone - you and all those entrusted to your care, and the community of the faithful as a whole, that is, the Church - to make a conscious, generous, whole-hearted act of faith in Jesus Christ our Lord. Our religious life must here and now be revitalised by this profession of faith. It must be a firm and resolute one, though always humble and diffident, like the faith of the man in St John's Gospel who had been blind from birth. When Jesus, whose kindness was as wonderful as His power, restored to him his sight, the man replied: "I believe, Lord."[10] Or like the faith of Martha in the same Gospel: "Yes, Lord, I have believed that thou art Christ, the Son of the living God, who art come into the world."[11] Or the faith which Simon, who was afterwards to be called Peter, expressed in words which are especially dear to Us: "Thou art Christ, the Son of the living God."[12] Why, then, do We presume to invite you to show your awareness of the Church and to make this explicit, though interior, act of faith?

24. There are indeed many reasons, and of necessity, it would seem, they all derive from the unparalleled circumstances in which the Church finds itself today.

---

[9] *Ph* 1:9.

[10] *Jn* 9:38.

[11] *Jn* 11:27.

[12] *Mt* 16:16.

The Present State of the Church

25. The Church needs to reflect upon itself and to become aware of its own extraordinary vitality. It must strive to gain a fuller understanding of itself if it is to do what it has to do and bring to the world the message of salvation and brotherly love. To use St Paul's phrase, it must experience the indwelling presence of Christ: "May Christ find a dwelling place through faith in your hearts."[13]

Deeply Rooted In A Changing World

26. As we all know, the Church is deeply rooted in the world. It exists in the world and draws its members from the world. It derives from it a wealth of human culture. It shares its vicissitudes and promotes its prosperity. But we also know that the modern world is in the grip of change and upheaval. It is undergoing developments which are having a profound influence on its outward way of life and habits of thought. The great advances made in science, technology, and social life, and the various currents of philosophical and political thought pervading modern society, are greatly influencing men's opinions and their spiritual and cultural pursuits.

Dangers and Their Remedy

The Church itself is being engulfed and shaken by this tidal wave of change, for however much men may be committed to the Church, they are deeply affected by the climate of the world. They run the risk of becoming confused, bewildered and alarmed, and this is a state of affairs which strikes at the very roots of the Church. It drives many people to adopt the most outlandish views. They imagine that the Church should abdicate its proper role, and adopt an entirely new and unprecedented mode of existence. Modernism might be cited as an example. This is an error which is still making its appearance under various new guises, wholly inconsistent with any genuine religious expression. It is surely an attempt on the

---

[13] *Ep* 3:17.

part of secular philosophies and secular trends to vitiate the true teaching and discipline of the Church of Christ.

An effective remedy is needed if all these dangers, which are prevalent in many quarters, are to be obviated, and We believe that such a remedy is to be found in an increased self-awareness on the part of the Church. The Church must get a clearer idea of what it really is in the mind of Jesus Christ as recorded and preserved in Sacred Scripture and in Apostolic Tradition, and interpreted and explained by the tradition of the Church under the inspiration and guidance of the Holy Spirit. Provided we implore the aid of the Spirit and show Him a ready obedience, He will certainly never fail to redeem Christ's promise: "But the Paraclete, the Holy Ghost, whom the Father will send in my name, he will teach you all things and bring all things to your mind, whatsoever I shall have said to you."[14]

27. The same could be said of the errors we see circulating within the Church itself and to which people are exposed who have only a partial understanding of the Church and its mission, and who do not pay close enough attention to divine revelation and the Church's Christ-given authority to teach.

Modern Bent of Mind

28. But the need for serious reflection on truths which are already well known is in close accordance with the genius and mentality of our contemporaries, who like to explore their minds in depth. They find mental repose in the secure grasp of truth, apprehended, as it were, in the light of conscience. Not that this method of enquiry is without serious risk. Famous philosophers have studied this activity of the human intellect and pronounced it to be its most perfect and highest function. They have actually gone so far as to maintain that it is the measure and source of reality, and this has led them to some abstruse, barren, absurd, and wholly fallacious conclusions. Nevertheless, this does not mean that the training of

---

[14] *Jn* 14:26.

the mind to scrutinise the truth which lies in the depth of its own awareness is not in itself an excellent thing. It is reckoned today as being the highest expression of modern culture. And if this mental discipline is carefully co-ordinated with that habit of mind whereby a man discovers objective truth, the investigation of one's conscious knowledge may well lead to a greater knowledge of oneself, one's dignity as a human being, one's intellectual powers and practical ability.

Self-Examination Well Under Way

29. It is a fact, moreover, that in recent years the Church has actually embarked on a deeper study of itself. Outstanding theologians have made an excellent contribution to this work. So have great scholars and intellectuals, the foremost theological schools, and pastoral and missionary societies. Successful experiments have been conducted in the religious field, and we have, above all, the memorable doctrinal statements issued by the popes.

30. It would take too long even to summarise the abundant theological literature dealing with the Church and produced by the Church in the course of the nineteenth and twentieth centuries. It would also take too long to pass in review all the documents issued by the Church's hierarchy and this Apostolic See on this monumental and important subject. Eminent theologians have been studying the subject ever since the Council of Trent sought to repair the damage resulting from the great crisis in the sixteenth century which separated so many members from the Church of Christ.

The Two Vatican Councils

Much progress has therefore been made. Suffice it here to refer to the relevant findings of the First Ecumenical Vatican Council. From these it is obvious that the doctrine concerning the Church is one which must claim the attention not only of pastors and teachers, but also of the faithful, and indeed of all Christians. This doctrine is a necessary stepping-stone to the understanding of Christ and His work. It is precisely because the Second Vatican Council has the task of dealing once more with the doctrine *de Ecclesia* and of defining it, that it has been called the continuation and complement of the First Vatican Council.

We do not wish to dilate further on this subject, as We must be brief and you are already well acquainted with it. It has been widely publicised within the Church today, both as matter for catechesis and for the spiritual life.

Leo XIII and Pius XII on the Church

There are, however, two documents which deserve special mention: the encyclical *Satis Cognitum*[15] of Pope Leo XIII, published in 1896, and the encyclical *Mystici Corporis*[16] of Pope Pius XII, published in 1943. These documents offer us ample and clear teaching concerning the subject of Our present discourse: that divine institution through which Christ continues His redemptive work in the world. Let it be enough to cite just the opening words of the second of these papal documents which has already become a highly authoritative text on the theology of the Church and a rich source of spiritual meditation on this work of divine mercy which concerns us all. Consider, then, this splendid utterance of Our predecessor:

"The doctrine of the Mystical Body of Christ, which is the Church, a doctrine revealed originally from the lips of the Redeemer Himself, and making manifest the inestimable boon of our most intimate union with so august a Head, has a surpassing splendour which commends it to the meditation of all who are moved by the divine Spirit, and with the light which it sheds on their minds, is a powerful stimulus to the salutary conduct which it enjoins."[17]

---

[15] *Acta Leonis XIII*, XVI (1896), 157-208.

[16] AAS XXXV (1943), 193-248.

[17] AAS XXXV (1943), 193.

31. We wish to take up this invitation and to repeat it in this encyclical, for We consider it timely and urgent and relevant to the needs of the Church in our day. With a richer understanding of the Mystical Body, we will be enabled to appreciate its theological significance and find in it a great source of spiritual strength. In this way we will notably increase our application to the task of fulfilling our own mission of serving mankind. In view of the vast literature on the subject of the Church and the fact that it is the principal topic engaging the attention of the Second Ecumenical Vatican Council, there should be no difficulty about this.

The Contribution of Scholars

Here We would like to pay special tribute to those brilliant scholars whose extremely competent works of theological research and exposition, undertaken in exemplary submission to the Church's teaching authority, have made such an expert and useful contribution to this subject, especially within recent years. They have carried on this work not only in the theological schools, but also in discussions with academicians and intellectuals, in popular writings in defence of the Christian truth, in the spiritual direction of the faithful, and in conversations with our separated brethren. In all this they have presented many and various illustrations of the doctrine on the Church, many of which are quite outstanding and exceptionally useful.

32. And so We are confident that the great work of the Council will continue to enjoy the help and light of the Holy Spirit, and will be brought to a successful conclusion through our readiness to follow His divine inspirations, our eagerness to inquire more fully and more deeply into the genuine teaching of Christ and its legitimate and necessary development in the course of history, and our earnest resolve to make of divine truth an argument for union, understanding, and harmony among men and not a reason for dividing them in sterile discussions and regrettable rivalries. Thus may the Council be a source of glory for God, joy for His Church, and edification for the world.

The Path Ahead

33. In this encyclical We are deliberately refraining from making any judgement of Our own on doctrinal issues concerning the Church which are at present under examination by the Council of which We are president. We wish to leave full liberty of investigation and discussion to this important and authoritative assembly. We will express Our own mind at the proper time and in the proper manner, as Our apostolic office of teacher and shepherd and head of the Church demands, and then Our greatest wish will be to have Our own decision in full accord with the judgement of the conciliar Fathers.

34. However, We cannot let this opportunity pass without alluding briefly to the salvific effects which We hope will result from the Council itself and from the efforts which, as We said above, the Church must make to come to a fuller and firmer awareness of itself. These results are the aims We set for Our apostolic ministry when We undertook its consoling yet tremendous responsibilities. They are, so to say, the very blueprint of Our pontificate, which We wish to describe to you, Venerable Brethren, in briefest outline, but in all sincerity, so as to gain your advice, support and co-operation. In opening Our heart to you, We realise that through you We are addressing all the sons of God's Church, and it is Our dearest hope that Our voice will be heard even by those who are outside the open fold of Christ.

Rediscovering the Mystical Body

35. The first benefit which We trust the Church will reap from a deepened self-awareness, is a renewed discovery of its vital bond of union with Christ. This is something which is perfectly well known, but it is supremely important and absolutely essential. It can never be sufficiently understood, meditated upon and preached. What shall We not say about this truth, which is the principal item, surely, of the whole of our religious heritage? Fortunately, you already have an excellent grasp of this doctrine, and here We would

add nothing further except to make a strenuous recommendation that you always attribute maximum importance to it and look upon it as a guiding principle both in your spiritual life and in your preaching of the word of God.

Consider the words of Our Predecessor, Pius XII, rather than Our own. In his memorable encyclical *Mystici Corporis* he wrote: "We must accustom ourselves to see Christ Himself in the Church. For it is indeed Christ who lives in the Church, and through her teaches, governs, and sanctifies; and it is also Christ who manifests Himself in manifold guise in the various members of His society."[18]

How gratifying and pleasant it is to dwell on the words of Sacred Scripture, the Fathers, Doctors and Saints, which come to our minds when we contemplate this wonderful article of faith. Was it not Jesus Himself who told us that He was the vine and we the branches?[19] Do we not have before us all the riches of St Paul's teaching, who never ceases to remind us that we "are all one person in Jesus Christ"?[20] He is always exhorting us to "grow up in him who is the head, even Christ, from whom the whole body...,"[21] and admonishes us that "Christ is all in all."[22]

As for the Doctors of the Church, We need only recall this passage from St Augustine: "Let us rejoice and give thanks that we have become not only Christians, but Christ. Do you understand, brothers, the grace of Christ our Head? Wonder at it, rejoice: we have become Christ. For if He is the Head, we are the members; He and we form the whole man . . . the fullness of Christ, therefore; the head and the members. What is the head and the members? Christ and the Church."[23]

---

[18] AAS XXXV (1943), 238.

[19] Cf. *Jn* 15:1 ff.

[20] *Ga* 3:28.

[21] *Ep* 4:15-16.

[22] *Col* 3:11.

[23] *In Io. tract.* 21. 8; PL 35. 1568.

Mature Faith: the Key

36. This, as we well know, is a mystery, the mystery of the Church. But if we give it our whole-hearted attention, inevitably we will gain much spiritual profit, and the Church of our day would seem to be in the greatest need of such spiritual profit. Christ's presence, His very life, will reveal its power and efficacy in our individual souls and in the whole Mystical Body; and this by the practice of a living and life-giving faith, so that, as St Paul said in the passage from which We have already quoted, "Christ may dwell through faith in your hearts."[24]

It is through faith that we gain this awareness of the mystery of the Church-mature faith, a faith lived out in our lives. Faith such as this gives us a sensus Ecclesiae, an awareness of the Church, and this is something with which the genuine Christian should be deeply imbued. He has been raised in the school of the divine word, nourished by the grace of the sacraments and the Paraclete's heavenly inspiration, trained in the practice of the virtues of the Gospel, and influenced by the Church's culture and community life. He has, moreover, the tremendous joy of sharing in the dignity of the royal priesthood granted to the people of God.[25]

The Hierarchy: an Instrument

37. The mystery of the Church is not a truth to be confined to the realms of speculative theology. It must be lived, so that the faithful may have a kind of intuitive experience of it, even before they come to understand it clearly. And the faithful as a community will indeed recognise that they belong to Christ's Mystical Body when they realise that a part of the ministry of the Church's hierarchy is to initiate men into the Christian way of life, to beget them,[26] teach them, sanctify them, and be their leaders. The hierarchy is a sort of instrument fashioned by Christ, which He Himself uses to

---

[24] *Ep* 3:17.

[25] Cf. *1 Pt* 2:9.

[26] Cf. *Ga* 4:19; *1 Co* 4:15.

communicate to His mystical members the marvellous gifts of truth and grace. He uses it, too, to impart an external, visible structure to the Mystical Body in its pilgrimage through the world, and to give it its sublime unity, its ability to perform its various tasks, its concerted multiplicity of form, and its spiritual beauty.

Images are powerless to convey to the mind an adequate notion of the reality and sublimity of this mystery, but having mentioned the image which St Paul used, that of the Mystical Body, We should also make mention of the image used by Christ, that of a building, of which He is Himself the architect and builder. Though He founded this building on a man who was naturally weak and frail, Christ transformed him into solid rock, never to be without God's marvellous support: "Upon this rock I will build my Church."[27]

38. If we can only stir up this awareness of the Church in ourselves and foster it in the faithful by the noble and pastoral art of education, many of the apparent difficulties which are today exercising the minds of students of ecclesiology will in fact be overcome. I mean such difficulties as how the Church can be at once both visible and spiritual, free and yet subject to discipline, claiming to be communal in character and yet organized on a sacred, hierarchical basis, already holy and yet still striving for holiness, at once both contemplative and active, and so on. All these matters will become clear through our actually living the Church's life. This is the best illustration and confirmation of its teaching.

Cultivating the Highest Spirituality

There is a further very great advantage that will result from this awareness of the Church: namely, the best type of spirituality, nourished by the reading of Sacred Scripture and the Church's holy Fathers and Doctors, and by everything else that can foster this awareness in the Church: systematic catechetical instruction, an active participation in the sacred liturgy - an incomparable school

---

[27] *Mt* 16:18.

of spirituality, with its words, signs and prayers - fervent, silent meditation on heavenly truths, and determined effort to cultivate the prayer of contemplation.

Indeed, the cultivation of Christian perfection must still be regarded as the richest source of the Church's spiritual strength. It is the means, so peculiarly its own, whereby the Church basks in the sunlight of Christ's Spirit. It is the Church's natural and necessary way of expressing its religious and social activity. It is the Church's surest defence and the cause of its constant renewal of strength amid the difficulties of the secular world.

Meaning of Baptism

39. Those who are baptised and by this means incorporated into Christ's Mystical Body, His Church, must attach the greatest importance to this event. They must be acutely aware of being raised to a higher status, of being reborn to a supernatural life, there to experience the happiness of being God's adopted sons, the special dignity of being Christ's brothers, the blessedness, the grace and the joy of the indwelling Holy Spirit.

They have indeed been called to a new kind of life, but they have lost nothing of their own humanity except the unhappy state of original sin. Rather, the humanity in them is now capable of bearing the fairest flowers of perfection and the most precious and holiest of fruits. To be a Christian, to have received holy Baptism, must not be looked upon as something of negligible importance. It must be something which thrills the baptised person to the very core of his being. He must look upon it with the eyes of the Christians of the early Church, as an "illumination" which draws down upon his soul the life-giving radiance of divine truth, opens heaven to him, and sheds upon this mortal life that light which enables him to walk as a child of the light toward the vision of God, the wellspring of eternal happiness.

40. It is easy to see what practical resolutions affecting ourselves and our ministry are encouraged by such considerations as these.

And we are happy to see that these resolutions are already being implemented everywhere in the Church and are being fostered by prudent and ardent religious zeal. We approve them, praise them, and confirm them with Our blessing.

II. THE RENEWAL

41. Our intense desire is to see the Church become what Christ intended it to be: one, holy, and entirely dedicated to the pursuit of that perfection to which Christ called it and for which He qualified it. In its pilgrimage through the world the Church must really strive to manifest that ideal of perfection envisaged for it by the divine Redeemer. Here, therefore, we have the greatest problem confronting the living Church. It is a problem which shows how powerful and effective the Church really is. It goads it into action, submits it to searching criticism and keeps it true to its purpose. It engenders in the Church prayer and compunction, repentance and hope, toil and confidence, the spirit of adventure and achievement.

It is a problem which arises from the very nature of the truths revealed by God and their special relevance to our lives as human beings. For without reference to Christ's teaching handed on by the Church, it is not possible for man to pass judgement on himself and his own nature, his former state of perfection and the ruinous consequences of original sin, his capacity for good and his need for help in desiring and achieving what is good, the importance and purpose of this present life, the good that he seeks or already possesses, how best to acquire perfection and holiness, and how to attain to the highest degree of perfection and completeness.

Hence the Church must be gripped with an intense and unfailing desire to learn the ways of the Lord. It is Our dearest wish that all those valuable discussions concerning Christian perfection which have gone on for so many centuries in the Church, shall once again receive the importance they deserve and arouse the faithful, not indeed to formulate new rules of spirituality, but to generate new energies in striving after the holiness which Christ has taught us. His own words and example, his guidance and assistance, have made it possible for us to know about this holiness and to desire it and achieve it. This method of spirituality which is confirmed by the custom and tradition of the Church, established by the united action of its members, and exemplified in the outstanding lives of the Saints.

And to Sanctify the World

42. The very external conditions in which the Church finds itself give added impetus to this striving for religious and moral perfection, for the Church cannot remain indifferent to or unaffected by the changes which take place in the world around. They influence, modify, and condition its course of action in all sorts of ways. As we know, the Church does not exist in isolation from the world. It lives in the world, and its members are consequently influenced and guided by the world. They imbibe its culture, are subject to its laws and adopt its customs. This intimate contact with the world is continually creating problems for the Church and at the present time these problems are extremely acute.

The Christian life, as encouraged and preserved by the Church, must resist every possible source of deception, contamination, or restriction of its freedom. It must guard against these things as it would guard against contamination by error or evil. Yet at the same time it must not only adapt itself to the forms of thought and living which a temporal environment induces, one might almost say imposes, on it-provided, of course, such forms are not incompatible with the basic principles of its religious and moral teaching-but it must also strive to approach these forms and to correct, ennoble, encourage, and sanctify them. And this demands of the Church a continual process of self-examination and re-appraisal of its external conduct. This in fact is what the present era is demanding of the Church with such insistence and earnestness.

Help From the Council

43. Here again the timing of this Council is most opportune. Its principal aim is to be pastoral in character, to renew the code of Canon Law and to make the practice of the Christian life easier, in so far as this can be done consistently with its divine nature.

Hence the Council is a great success even now, before the promulgation of most of the decrees expected of it. It is stirring the minds of pastors and faithful alike and inspiring them to preserve and increase the supernatural integrity of the Christian life. It is serving as a reminder to everyone of his duty in conscience to ensure that his daily conduct bears this authentic stamp firmly imprinted upon it. It is encouraging the remiss to become good, the good to become better. These, in their turn, are being inspired with the spirit of generosity; the generous are being drawn toward sanctity. In addition, the Council is revealing new ways of acquiring holiness. Love is sharpened to the point of inventiveness, and we find a new enthusiasm for a life of virtue and Christian heroism.

44. It will be for the Council, naturally, to decide what reforms are to be introduced into the Church's legislation and discipline. The post-conciliar committees, or commissions - especially the Commission for the Revision of Canon Law, which has already been set up - will concern themselves with the task of formulating in concrete terms the recommendations of the Ecumenical Synod. It will be your duty, therefore, Venerable Brethren, to indicate to us what decisions are required for purifying and rejuvenating the Church's image. Let Us, for Our part, give public expression once again to this resolve of Ours to do all We can to sponsor this reform.

How often in past centuries has the determination to instigate reforms been associated with the holding of ecumenical councils! Let it be so once more; but this time not with a view to removing any specific heresies concerning the Church, or to remedying any public disorders - for disorders of this sort have not, thank God, raised their head in our midst - but rather with a view to infusing fresh spiritual vigour into Christ's Mystical Body considered as a visible society, and to purifying it from the defects of many of its members and urging it on to the attainment of new virtue.

The Kind of Reform Necessary

45. In order, with God's help, to achieve this result, allow Us to put before you certain considerations designed to facilitate such reforms, to give you the necessary courage to instigate them - for they are bound to involve you in certain sacrifices - and to outline some general principles for their more effective implementation.

Church's Nature Not Involved

46. First We must lay down a few rules to guide us in the work of reform. Obviously, there can be no question of reforming the essential nature of the Church or its basic and necessary structure. To use the word reform in that context would be to misuse it completely. We cannot brand the holy and beloved Church of God with the mark of infidelity. We must consider our membership in it as one of our greatest blessings. It testifies to our spirit "that we are the children of God."[28] No, it is not pride nor arrogance nor obstinacy nor stupidity nor folly that makes us so sure of being living, genuine members of Christ's Body, the authentic heirs of His Gospel, the lawful successors of the Apostles. It is a firm faith, a joyous conviction. We hold in our possession that great heritage of truth and holiness which characterises the Catholic Church of the present day, preserving intact the living heritage of the original apostolic tradition.

That is our boast, if you like. It is rather our reason for giving thanks continually to God.[29] It is also the reason why we feel ourselves bound by a graver responsibility before God, to whom we are accountable for so great a benefit, and before the Church in which we must arouse this same conviction together with the desire and resolve to guard this treasure, this "deposit," as St Paul calls it.[30] We have a responsibility too toward our separated brothers and toward all men, so that all may share with us the gift of God.

Restoration, But Not Reduction

47. In this context, therefore, when we speak about reform we are not concerned to change things, but to preserve all the more resolutely the characteristic features which Christ has impressed on His Church. Or rather, we are concerned to restore to the Church that ideal of perfection and beauty that corresponds to its original

---

[28] *Rm* 8:16.

[29] Cf. *Ep* 5:20.

[30] Cf. *1 Tm* 6:20.

image, and that is at the same time consistent with its necessary, normal and legitimate growth from its original, embryonic form into its present structure.

No one should deceive himself into thinking that the Church which has now become a vast, magnificent, and majestic temple built to the glory of God, should be reduced to the modest proportions which it had in its earliest days, as though this minimal form were the only one that is genuine and lawful. Nor should one conceive the desire of renewing the whole structure of the Church just by taking account of the special spiritual gifts (charism) of some of its members. Some imagine that the only genuine renewal of the Church is one which is born from the ideas of a few, admittedly zealous, people who not infrequently consider themselves divinely inspired. Their vain dreams of the wrong sort of renewal could easily defile the very shape which the Church ought to have.

We must love and serve the Church as it is, wisely seeking to understand its history and to discover with humility the will of God who guides and assists it, even when He permits human weakness to eclipse the splendour of its countenance and the holiness of its activity. It is precisely this holiness and splendour which we are endeavouring to discover and promote.

Avoid Over-Adapting

48. We must strengthen these convictions in ourselves if we are also to avoid another danger which the desire for reform can produce, not so much in us pastors, who are restrained by the proper awareness of our sacred duty, as in many of the faithful, who think that the reform of the Church should consist principally in adapting its way of thinking and acting to the customs and temper of the modern secular world. The fascination of worldly life today is very powerful indeed, and many people regard conformity to it as an inescapable and indeed a wise course to take. Hence, those who are not deeply rooted in the faith and in the observance of the Church's laws, readily imagine that the time is ripe to adjust themselves to

worldly standards of living, on the assumption that these are the best and only possible ones for a Christian to adopt.

This craving for uniformity is observable even in the realm of philosophy (it is extraordinary how much weight is attached to fashion in a province where the mind ought to be free and independent, anxious only to arrive at the truth, and bowing to the authority of none but proved masters). It is observable also in the realm of ethics, making it more and more perplexing and difficult to define moral rectitude and the right conduct of life.

False Philosophies

49. In addition we are confronted with the doctrine of Naturalism, which attempts to undermine the fundamental conception of Christianity. Relativism, too, seeks to justify everything, and treats all things as of equal value. It assails the absolute character of Christian principles.

We are also confronted with the growing tendency to prune away from the Christian life everything that requires effort or causes inconvenience. It rejects as vain and futile the practice of Christian asceticism and the contemplation of the things of God.

Indeed, sometimes even the apostolic desire for a ready passport into secular society and the determination to make oneself acceptable to men and particularly to the youth of today, prompts certain people to lay aside the principles which characterise our faith and to reject the sort of dignity which gives meaning and force to our determination to make contact with others and makes our teaching effective. Is it not, perhaps, true that some of the younger clergy and religious, in their laudable endeavour to come closer to the masses and to particular groups, aim at becoming like them rather than different from them? By this worthless imitation they forfeit the real value and effectiveness of their endeavours.

We must be in the world, but not of it. These important words of Christ are especially relevant at the present time, difficult though they may be to put into practice. It will be well for us if Christ, who lives always to make intercession for us,[31] includes us moderns in the wonderful prayer He addressed to His heavenly Father: "I pray not that thou shouldst take them out of the world, but that thou shouldst keep them from evil."[32]

Aggiornamento: the Guiding Principle

50. The purpose of this exhortation of Ours is not to lend substance to the belief that perfection consists in rigidly adhering to the methods adopted by the Church in the past and refusing to countenance the practical measures commonly thought to be in accord with the character of our time. These measures can be put to the test. We cannot forget Pope John XXIII's word "aggiornamento" which We have adopted as expressing the aim and object of Our own pontificate. Besides ratifying it and confirming it as the guiding principle of the Ecumenical Council, We want to bring it to the notice of the whole Church. It should prove a stimulus to the Church to increase its ever growing vitality and its ability to take stock of itself and give careful consideration to the signs of the times, always and everywhere "proving all things and holding fast that which is good"[33] with the enthusiasm of youth.

Obedience to Christ's Will

51. But let Us repeat once again for our common admonition and profit: the Church will rediscover its youthful vitality not so much by changing its external legislation, as by submitting to the obedience of Christ and observing the laws which the Church lays upon itself with the intention of following in Christ's footsteps. Herein lies the secret of the Church's renewal, its *metanoia*, to use the Greek term, its practice of perfection.

---

[31] Cf. *Heb* 7:25.

[32] *Jn* 17:15.

[33] Cf. *1 Th* 5:21.

Not Less, Perhaps More, Required

Even though the Church, in the reliance which it places on the liberty of the modern Christian with his increased awareness of his duties and his greater maturity and practical wisdom in fulfilling them, may make certain of its laws or precepts easier to observe, nevertheless the law retains its essential binding force. The Christian way of life as set forth and interpreted by the Church in its prudent legislation, demands a not inconsiderable degree of loyalty, perseverance and self-sacrifice. It constrains us, as it were, to take the "narrow way" recommended by Our Saviour.[34] It will not require less of us modern Christians than in the past; it may very well require more. It will require a prompt obedience, no less necessary and difficult now than formerly, but it will be all the more meritorious in that it is inspired more by supernatural motives than by natural ones. Conformity to the spirit of the world, the rejection of the rules of Christian asceticism, indifference in the face of the laxity of contemporary morals, emancipation from the authority of wise and lawful superiors, apathy concerning the contradictory forms of modern thought - these are not the things that can give vigour to the Church and fit it to receive the power and strength of the Holy Spirit's gifts. These are not the things which strengthen the Church in its true following of Christ. They neither inject into the Church the watchful spirit of brotherly love, nor do they increase its ability to communicate its message. The only things which can bring these blessings on the Church are the following: the determination to live in accordance with divine grace, faithfulness to the Gospel of Christ, unity in the ranks of the sacred hierarchy and among Christian communities. The follower of Christ is not pliant and cowardly, but loyal and strong.

52. We realise that it would take Us too long to describe here, even in barest outline, the way in which the Christian life should be lived today, and We have no intention of embarking on such an undertaking now. In any case, you are well aware of the moral needs of our time, and you will not cease in your efforts to bring the

---

[34] Cf. *Mt* 7:13.

faithful to a realisation of the dignity, the purity and the seriousness of the Christian life. Nor will you fail to do all you can to denounce, even publicly, the moral dangers and vices of our age. We all remember the solemn exhortations uttered in Holy Scripture: "I know thy works and thy labour and thy patience and how thou canst not bear them that are evil."[35] These words will inspire us to become watchful and diligent pastors. The Ecumenical Council will give us new and profitable instructions, and we should be preparing ourselves even now to welcome them and to put them into effect.

Two Fundamental Gospel Precepts

53. There are, however, two special points We feel constrained to mention. They have to do with needs and duties which seem to Us to be paramount, and they provide matter for reflection on the general lines of the renewal of ecclesiastical life.

The Spirit of Poverty

54. The first of them is the spirit of poverty, or rather, the zeal for preserving this spirit. We presume to mention it explicitly in this encyclical letter because of Our conviction of the prominence which this precept receives in Christ's holy Gospel. It is a fundamental element of that divine plan by which we are destined to win the kingdom of God, and yet it is greatly jeopardised by the modern trend to set so much store by wealth.

The zeal for the spirit of poverty is vitally necessary if we are to realise the many failures and mistakes we have made in the past, and learn the principle on which we must now base our way of life and how best to proclaim the religion of Christ.

To Be Subject to New Regulations

One further reason for Our mentioning it here is the difficulty we all find in practicing it. It is Our intention to issue special

[35] *Rv* 2:2.

canonical regulations on this subject, but We do ask you, Venerable Brethren, for the support of your agreement, your counsel and your example. It is your task to interpret with authority the movements and inspirations of the Holy Spirit in the Church, and We rely on you to make clear to pastors and people how the spirit of poverty should regulate everything they do and say. As the Apostle Paul admonished Us: "Let this mind be in you, which was also in Christ Jesus."[36] We rely on you to indicate to us what decisions and regulations we should together make binding on the Church, so that we may base our confidence more on the help of God and on spiritual values, than on fallible, human means. The directives we need are such as will teach us and the men of this era that spiritual goods far outweigh economic goods, the possession and use of which should be regulated and subordinated to the conduct and advantage of our apostolic mission.

No Conflict with Economic Realities

55. The spirit of poverty is a special mark of Christ's Gospel. This passing reference to its necessity and excellence does not, however, relieve Us of Our obligation of pointing out that zeal for poverty is no obstacle to the proper understanding and rightful application of the important laws of economics. This is a subject which has made great strides within recent years. It has been responsible for the progress of civilisation, especially in its human and social aspects. But We consider that the inner freedom which results from zeal for evangelical poverty makes us in fact more sensitive to the human aspects of economic questions, and better fitted to understand them. We can pass, where necessary, a calm and often severe judgement on wealth and on the luxuries of life. We can come promptly and generously to the aid of those in need, and do our utmost to ensure that wealth, far from being a source of conflict, selfishness and pride amongst men, shall be used justly and equitably for the good of all, and distributed with greater foresight. In all that concerns these external goods-goods which are indeed inferior

---

[36] *Ph* 2:5.

to those that are spiritual and eternal, but which are nevertheless necessary in this present life-the student of the Gospel can come to a prudent decision. He has a real, human contribution to make in this field. We are most keenly interested in science, technology, and especially in work. The bread which they produce is sacred, whether destined for the table or the altar. This is the Church's traditional social teaching, and it leaves no room for doubt. It is a salutary doctrine. We readily seize this opportunity of confirming it by Our own authority.

Supreme Position of Charity

56. The other point We wish to raise has to do with the cultivation of charity, a subject, surely, which is already of deepest concern to you, for charity is the very heart and centre of the plan of God's providence as revealed in both the Old and New Testament. Are We not right in saying that charity is the goal of the Church's practice of the spiritual life? Is it not true to say that the more perfect and more joyful realisation of charity is the goal of all theological study and of the practice of Christian piety? Both these things encourage Us to meditate on the scriptural and sacramental treasures of which the Church is heir, guardian, mistress, and minister.

In full agreement with Our predecessors, with those saints whom our age has given to the Church on earth and in heaven, and with the devout instincts of the faithful, We are convinced that charity should today assume its rightful, foremost position in the scale of religious and moral values - and not just in theory, but in the practice of the Christian life. And this applies not only to the charity we show toward God who has poured out the abundance of His love upon us, but also to the charity which we in turn should lavish on our brothers, the whole human race.

Charity is the key to everything. It sets all to rights. There is nothing which charity cannot achieve and renew. Charity "beareth all things, believeth all things, hopeth all things, endureth all things."[37] Who is there among us who does not realise this? And since we realise it, is not this the time to put it into practice?

Mary, a Most Loving Teacher

57. This ideal of Christian perfection that We have set before you - a lofty, yet a lowly one - puts Us in mind of Mary, the holiest of Virgins, who reflects the ideal most perfectly and most wonderfully in her own person. Her life on earth was in fullest accord with this ideal, and now in heaven she enjoys its glory and blessedness. Devotion to the Mother of God is happily flourishing in the Church in this day and age, and We gladly take this opportunity of expressing Our admiration for Mary, the Holy Virgin Mother of Christ, the Mother of God and men, the model of Christian perfection, the mirror of true virtue, the pride of our humanity.

We regard devotion to the Mother of God as of paramount importance in living the life of the Gospel. When We made Our pilgrimage to the Holy Places, it was Our dearest wish to learn from her the lesson of true Christianity - from her who is the most blessed, lovable, humble and unsullied of creatures, privileged as she was to give human flesh in its original innocence and beauty to the eternal Word of God.

And now, Venerable Brethren, while discussing with you the spiritual and moral renewal of the Church's life, it is to her that We turn Our imploring gaze, for she is a most loving teacher of the way in which we must live.

---

[37] *1 Co* 13:7.

III. THE DIALOGUE

58. Under this third heading we must examine the mental attitude which the Catholic Church must adopt regarding the contemporary world. What contacts ought it to make at the present time with human society? - seeing that the Church's ever-increasing self-awareness and its struggle to model itself on Christ's ideal can only result in its acting and thinking quite differently from the world around it, which it is nevertheless striving to influence.

Motives for Dialogue

59. The Gospel clearly warns us of this difference and the need to keep ourselves distinct from the world. By the world, here, is meant either those human beings who are opposed to the light of faith and the gift of grace, those whose naive optimism betrays them into thinking that their own energies suffice to win them complete, lasting, and gainful prosperity, or, finally, those who take refuge in an aggressively pessimistic outlook on life and maintain that their vices, weaknesses and moral ailments are inevitable, incurable, or perhaps even desirable as sure manifestations of personal freedom and sincerity.

The Gospel of Christ recognises the existence of human infirmities. It recognises and denounces them with penetrating and often fierce sincerity. Yet it also understands them and cures them. It does not cherish the illusion that man is naturally good and self-sufficient, and needs only the ability to express himself as he pleases. Nor does it countenance a despairing acquiescence in the irremedial corruption of human nature. Christ's Gospel is light, newness, strength, salvation, and rebirth. It brings to birth a new and different kind of life, the marvels of which are proclaimed in the pages of the New Testament. Hence the admonition which St Paul gives: "Do not be conformed to this world, but be reformed in the newness of your mind, that you may prove what is the good and the acceptable and the perfect will of God".[38]

---

[38] *Rm* 12:2.

60. This difference between the Christian and the worldly life also arises from the fact that we are conscious of having been truly justified. Justification is produced in us by our sharing in the paschal mystery, particularly in Baptism, which is truly a rebirth, as St Paul teaches: "All who are baptised in Christ Jesus are baptised in his death. For we are buried together with him by baptism into death: that as Christ is risen from the dead by the glory of the Father, so we also may walk in newness of life."[39]

61. The modern Christian will do well, therefore, to reflect on this special and marvellous kind of life. He will thus be enabled to rejoice in the dignity that is his, to avoid the plague of human wretchedness which is everywhere around him, and to escape the seduction of human glory.

62. The Apostle of the Gentiles had this to say to the Christian of his day: "Bear not the yoke with unbelievers. For what participation hath justice with injustice? Or what fellowship hath light with darkness? . . . Or what part hath the faithful with the unbeliever?"[40] Hence the duty of modern educators and teachers in the Church of reminding young Catholics of their privileged position and of their obligation to live in the world, but not as the world lives. As Jesus Christ said in His prayer for His apostles: "I pray not that thou shouldst take them out of the world, but that thou shouldst keep them from evil. They are not of the world, as I also am not of the world."[41] Church makes this prayer its own.

Not Aloof, but Concerned and Loving

63. The fact that we are distinct from the world does not mean that we are entirely separated from it. Nor does it mean that we are indifferent to it, afraid of it, or contemptuous of it. When the Church distinguishes itself from humanity, it does so not in order to oppose it, but to come closer to it. A physician who realises the

---

[39] *Rm* 6:3-4.

[40] *2 Co* 6:14-15.

[41] *Jn* 17:15-16.

danger of disease, protects himself and others from it, but at the same time he strives to cure those who have contracted it. The Church does the same thing. It does not regard God's mercy as an exclusive privilege, nor does the greatness of the privilege it enjoys make it feel unconcerned for those who do not share it. On the contrary, it finds in its own salvation an argument for showing more concern and more love for those who live close at hand, or to whom it can go in its endeavour to make all alike share the blessing of salvation.

The Term Explained

64. If, as We said, the Church realises what is God's will in its regard, it will gain for itself a great store of energy, and in addition will conceive the need for pouring out this energy in the service of all men. It will have a clear awareness of a mission received from God, of a message to be spread far and wide. Here lies the source of our evangelical duty, our mandate to teach all nations, and our apostolic endeavour to strive for the eternal salvation of all men. Merely to remain true to the faith is not enough. Certainly we must preserve and defend the treasure of truth and grace that we have inherited through Christian tradition. As St Paul said, "keep that which is committed to thy trust."[42] But neither the preservation nor the defence of the faith exhausts the duty of the Church in regard to the gifts it has been given. The very nature of the gifts which Christ has given the Church demands that they be extended to others and shared with others. This must be obvious from the words: "Going, therefore, teach ye all nations,"[43] Christ's final command to His apostles. The word apostle implies a mission from which there is no escaping.

---

[42] *1 Tm* 6:20.
[43] *Mt* 28:19.

To this internal drive of charity which seeks expression in the external gift of charity, We will apply the word "dialogue".

65. The Church must enter into dialogue with the world in which it lives. It has something to say, a message to give, a communication to make.

66. We are fully aware that it is the intention of the Council to consider and investigate this special and important aspect of the Church's life, and We have no wish to steal its thunder. The Council Fathers must be free to discuss these subjects in detail. Our only concern, Venerable Brethren, is to propose certain points for your consideration before the beginning of the third session, so that we may all gain a clearer understanding of the compelling motives for the Church's dialogue, the methods to be followed and the end in view. Our purpose is to win souls, not to settle questions definitively.

Papal Precedents

67. In fact no other course is open to Us in view of Our conviction that it is this kind of dialogue that will characterise Our apostolic ministry. From Our predecessors of the past century We have inherited a pastoral outlook and a pastoral approach. Our first teacher is that great and wise Pope Leo XIII, who, like the prudent scribe in the Gospel, resembled a householder "who bringeth forth out of his treasure new things and old."[44] With all the dignity of the magisterial authority of the Holy See, he devoted himself wholeheartedly to finding a Christian solution to the problems of this modern age. Our other teachers are his successors, who, as you know, followed closely in his footsteps.

68. How truly wonderful is the inheritance of doctrinal riches bequeathed to Us by Our predecessors, and especially by Pius XI and Pius XII! Providentially they strove to bridge, as it were, the gap between divine and human wisdom, using not the language of

---

[44] *Mt* 13:52.

the textbook, but the ordinary language of contemporary speech. And what was this apostolic endeavour of theirs if not a dialogue?

As for Our immediate predecessor, John XXIII, he laboured with masterly assurance to bring divine truths as far as may be within the reach of the experience and understanding of modern man. Was not the Council itself given a pastoral orientation, and does it not rightly strive to inject the Christian message into the stream of modern thought, and into the language, culture, customs, and sensibilities of man as he lives in the spiritual turmoil of this modern world? Before we can convert the world - as the very condition of converting the world - we must approach it and speak to it.

69. Reluctant as we are to speak of Ourself and to draw attention to Ourself, We feel compelled, in presenting Ourself to the college of bishops and to the Christian people, to speak of Our resolve to persevere in this endeavour. We will strive, so far as Our weakness permits and God gives Us the grace, to approach the world in which God has destined Us to live. We will approach it with reverence, persistence, and love, in an effort to get to know it and to offer it the gifts of truth and grace of which God has made Us custodian. We will strive to make the world share in the divine redemption and in the hope which inspires Us. Engraven on Our heart are those words of Christ which We would humbly but resolutely make Our own: "For God sent not his Son into the world to judge the world, but that the world may be saved by him."[45]

The Dialogue of Salvation

70. Here, then, Venerable Brethren, is the noble origin of this dialogue: in the mind of God Himself. Religion of its very nature is a certain relationship between God and man. It finds its expression in prayer; and prayer is a dialogue. Revelation, too, that supernatural link which God has established with man, can likewise be looked upon as a dialogue. In the Incarnation and in the Gospel it is God's

---

[45] *Jn* 3:17.

Word that speaks to us. That fatherly, sacred dialogue between God and man, broken off at the time of Adam's unhappy fall, has since, in the course of history, been restored. Indeed, the whole history of man's salvation is one long, varied dialogue, which marvellously begins with God and which He prolongs with men in so many different ways.

In Christ's "conversation"[46] with men, God reveals something of Himself, of the mystery of His own life, of His own unique essence and trinity of persons. At the same time He tells us how He wishes to be known: as Love pure and simple; and how He wishes to be honoured and served: His supreme commandment is love. Child and mystic, both are called to take part in this unfailing, trustful dialogue; and the mystic finds there the fullest scope for his spiritual powers.

Sheds Light On New Dialogue

71. This relationship, this dialogue, which God the Father initiated and established with us through Christ in the Holy Spirit, is a very real one, even though it is difficult to express in words. We must examine it closely if we want to understand the relationship which we, the Church, should establish and foster with the human race.

Ours the Initiative

72. God Himself took the initiative in the dialogue of salvation. "He hath first loved us."[47] We, therefore, must be the first to ask for a dialogue with men, without waiting to be summoned to it by others.

Love the Inducement

73. The dialogue of salvation sprang from the goodness and the love of God. "God so loved the world as to give His only begotten

---

[46] Cf. *Ba* 3:38.
[47] *1 Jn* 4:10.

Son."[48] Our inducement, therefore, to enter into this dialogue must be nothing other than a love which is ardent and sincere.

Neither Limited, Self-Seeking, Nor Coercive

74. The dialogue of salvation did not depend on the merits of those with whom it was initiated, nor on the results it would be likely to achieve. "They that are whole need not the physician."[49] Neither, therefore, should we set limits to our dialogue or seek in it our own advantage.

75. No physical pressure was brought on anyone to accept the dialogue of salvation; far from it. It was an appeal of love. True, it imposed a serious obligation on those toward whom it was directed[50] but it left them free to respond to it or to reject it. Christ adapted the number of His miracles[51] and their demonstrative force to the dispositions and good will of His hearers[52] so as to help them to consent freely to the revelation they were given and not to forfeit the reward for their consent.

Hence although the truth we have to proclaim is certain and the salvation necessary, we dare not entertain any thoughts of external coercion. Instead we will use the legitimate means of human friendliness, interior persuasion, and ordinary conversation. We will offer the gift of salvation while respecting the personal and civic rights of the individual.

But Universal

76. The dialogue of salvation was made accessible to all. It applied to everyone without distinction.[53] Hence our dialogue too should

---

[48] *Jn* 3:16.
[49] *Lk* 5:31.
[50] Cf. *Mt* 11:21.
[51] Cf. *Mt* 12:38 ff.
[52] Cf. *Mt* 13:13 ff.
[53] Cf. *Col* 3:11.

be as universal as we can make it. That is to say, it must be catholic, made relevant to everyone, excluding only those who utterly reject it or only pretend to be willing to accept it.

And Persevering

77. Before it could be completely successful the dialogue of salvation had normally to begin in small things. It progressed gradually step by step.[54] Our dialogue too must take cognizance of the slowness of human and historical development, and wait for the hour when God may make it effective. We should not however on that account postpone until tomorrow what we can accomplish today. We should be eager for the opportune moment and sense the preciousness of time.[55] Today, every day, should see a renewal of our dialogue. We, rather than those to whom it is directed, should take the initiative.

Dialogue As A Method

78. Clearly, relationships between the Church and the world can be effective in a great variety of ways. The Church could perhaps justifiably reduce such contacts to a minimum, on the plea that it wishes to isolate itself from secular society. It might content itself with conducting an inquiry into the evils current in secular society, condemning them publicly, and fighting a crusade against them. On the other hand, it might approach secular society with a view to exercising a preponderant influence over it, and subjecting it to a theocratic power; and so on.

Best of Possible Approaches

But it seems to Us that the sort of relationship for the Church to establish with the world should be more in the nature of a dialogue, though theoretically other methods are not excluded. We do not mean unrealistic dialogue. It must be adapted to the intelligences

---

[54] Cf. *Mt* 13:31.

[55] Cf. *Ep* 5:16.

of those to whom it is addressed, and it must take account of the circumstances. Dialogue with children is not the same as dialogue with adults, nor is dialogue with Christians the same as dialogue with non-believers. But this method of approach is demanded nowadays by the prevalent understanding of the relationship between the sacred and the profane. It is demanded by the dynamic course of action which is changing the face of modern society. It is demanded by the pluralism of society, and by the maturity man has reached in this day and age. Be he religious or not, his secular education has enabled him to think and speak, and conduct a dialogue with dignity.

79. Moreover, the very fact that he engages in a dialogue of this sort is proof of his consideration and esteem for others, his understanding and his kindness. He detests bigotry and prejudice, malicious and indiscriminate hostility, and empty, boastful speech.

If, in our desire to respect a man's freedom and dignity, his conversion to the true faith is not the immediate object of our dialogue with him, we nevertheless try to help him and to dispose him for a fuller sharing of ideas and convictions.

80. Our dialogue, therefore, presupposes that there exists in us a state of mind which we wish to communicate and to foster in those around us. It is the state of mind which characterises the man who realises the seriousness of the apostolic mission and who sees his own salvation as inseparable from the salvation of others. His constant endeavour is to get everyone talking about the message which it has been given to him to communicate.

Its Proper Characteristics

81. Dialogue, therefore, is a recognised method of the apostolate. It is a way of making spiritual contact. It should however have the following characteristics:

1) Clarity before all else; the dialogue demands that what is said should be intelligible. We can think of it as a kind of thought

transfusion. It is an invitation to the exercise and development of the highest spiritual and mental powers a man possesses. This fact alone would suffice to make such dialogue rank among the greatest manifestations of human activity and culture. In order to satisfy this first requirement, all of us who feel the spur of the apostolate should examine closely the kind of speech we use. Is it easy to understand? Can it be grasped by ordinary people? Is it current idiom?

2) Our dialogue must be accompanied by that meekness which Christ bade us learn from Himself: "Learn of me, for I am meek and humble of heart."[56] It would indeed be a disgrace if our dialogue were marked by arrogance, the use of bared words or offensive bitterness. What gives it its authority is the fact that it affirms the truth, shares with others the gifts of charity, is itself an example of virtue, avoids peremptory language, makes no demands. It is peaceful, has no use for extreme methods, is patient under contradiction and inclines towards generosity.

3) Confidence is also necessary; confidence not only in the power of one's own words, but also in the good will of both parties to the dialogue. Hence dialogue promotes intimacy and friendship on both sides. It unites them in a mutual adherence to the Good, and thus excludes all self-seeking.

4) Finally, the prudence of a teacher who is most careful to make allowances for the psychological and moral circumstances of his hearer,[57] particularly if he is a child, unprepared, suspicious or hostile. The person who speaks is always at pains to learn the sensitivities of his audience, and if reason demands it, he adapts himself and the manner of his presentation to the susceptibilities and the degree of intelligence of his hearers.

82. In a dialogue conducted with this kind of foresight, truth is wedded to charity and understanding to love.

---

[56] *Mt* 11:29.

[57] *Mt* 7:6.

Deeper Knowledge Through Wider Exposure

83. And that is not all. For it becomes obvious in a dialogue that there are various ways of coming to the light of faith and it is possible to make them all converge on the same goal. However divergent these ways may be, they can often serve to complete each other. They encourage us to think on different lines. They force us to go more deeply into the subject of our investigations and to find better ways of expressing ourselves. It will be a slow process of thought, but it will result in the discovery of elements of truth in the opinion of others and make us want to express our teaching with great fairness. It will be set to our credit that we expound our doctrine in such a way that others can respond to it, if they will, and assimilate it gradually. It will make us wise; it will make us teachers.

Modes of Dialogue

84. Consider now the form which the dialogue of salvation takes, and the manner of exposition.

85. It has many forms. If necessary it takes account of actual experience. It chooses appropriate means. It is unencumbered by prejudice. It does not hold fast to forms of expression which have lost their meaning and can no longer stir men's minds.

The Crucial Question

86. We are faced here with a serious problem: how is the Church to adapt its mission to the particular age, environment, educational and social conditions of men's lives?

87. To what extent should the Church adapt itself to the historical and local circumstances in which it has to exercise its mission? How is it to guard against the danger of relativism which would make it untrue to its own dogmas and moral principles? And yet how can it fit itself to approach all men and bring salvation to all,

becoming on the example of the Apostle Paul "all things to all men," that all may be saved?[58]

Preliminary Conditions

Since the world cannot be saved from the outside, we must first of all identify ourselves with those to whom we would bring the Christian message - like the Word of God who Himself became a man. Next we must forego all privilege and the use of unintelligible language, and adopt the way of life of ordinary people in all that is human and honourable. Indeed, we must adopt the way of life of the most humble people, if we wish to be listened to and understood. Then, before speaking, we must take great care to listen not only to what men say, but more especially to what they have it in their hearts to say. Only then will we understand them and respect them, and even, as far as possible, agree with them.

Furthermore, if we want to be men's pastors, fathers and teachers, we must also behave as their brothers. Dialogue thrives on friendship, and most especially on service. All this we must remember and strive to put into practice on the example and precept of Christ.[59]

Dangers

88. But the danger remains. Indeed, the worker in the apostolate is under constant fire. The desire to come together as brothers must not lead to a watering down or whittling away of truth. Our dialogue must not weaken our attachment to our faith. Our apostolate must not make vague compromises concerning the principles which regulate and govern the profession of the Christian faith both in theory and in practice.

An immoderate desire to make peace and sink differences at all costs (irenism and syncretism) is ultimately nothing more than scepticism about the power and content of the Word of God

---

[58] *1 Co* 9:22.
[59] Cf. *Jn* 13:14-17.

which we desire to preach. The effective apostle is the man who is completely faithful to Christ's teaching. He alone can remain unaffected by the errors of the world around him, the man who lives his Christian life to the full.

Direction from the Council

89. We believe that when the Ecumenical Council comes to deal with the problems relating to the Church's activity in the modern world, it will give the doctrinal and practical rules needed for the proper conduct of our dialogue with our contemporaries. We believe too that in matters relating to the Church's actual apostolic mission and the many changing circumstances in which it is exercised, the supreme authority of the Church will in every instance determine wise, effective and clear aims, principles, and methods, so that a lively and effective dialogue may be assured and lasting.

Preaching the Primary Apostolate

90. However, leaving aside this aspect of the matter, We want to stress once more the very important place that preaching still has, especially in the modern Catholic apostolate and in connection with the dialogue which is Our present concern. No other form of communication can take its place; not even the exceptionally powerful and effective means provided by modern technology: the press, radio and television.

In effect, the apostolate and sacred preaching are more or less synonymous terms. Preaching is the primary apostolate. Our ministry, Venerable Brethren, is before all else the ministry of the Word. We are well aware of this, but it is good to remind ourselves of it at the present time so as to give the right orientation to our pastoral activities. We must return to the study, not of human eloquence of empty rhetoric, but of the genuine art of proclaiming the Word of God.

91. We must search for the principles which make for simplicity, clarity, effectiveness and authority, and so overcome our natural ineptitude in the use of this great and mysterious instrument of the divine Word, and be a worthy match for those whose skill in the use of words makes them so influential in the world today and gives them access to the organs of public opinion. We must pray to the Lord for this vital, soul-stirring gift,[60] that we may be fit instruments in the work of really and effectively preaching the faith,[61] and that our message may reach to the ends of the earth.[62]

May we carry out intelligently and zealously everything that the Council's Constitution on the Sacred Liturgy has prescribed regarding the ministry of the Word. And may the instruction we give our Christian people and others, insofar as it is possible, be skilfully expressed, carefully thought out, and zealously imparted. May it be supported by the evidence of real virtue. Progress must be its aim. It must concern itself with imparting a sure faith, a realisation of the intimate connection between God's Word and man's life, and the enjoyment of some ray of divine light.

The Church in Dialogue

92. Finally We must say something about those to whom our dialogue is addressed; but even here We have no wish to forestall the decisions of the Council, which, please God, will soon be made known.

Message for Everyone

93. Speaking generally of the dialogue which the Church of today must take up with a great renewal of fervour, We would say that it must be readily conducted with all men of good will both inside and outside the Church.

---

[60] Cf. *Jr* 1:6.

[61] Cf. *Rm* 10:17.

[62] Cf. *Ps* 18:5, *Rm* 10:18.

94. The Church can regard no one as excluded from its motherly embrace, no one as outside the scope of its motherly care. It has no enemies except those who wish to make themselves such. Its catholicity is no idle boast. It was not for nothing that it received its mission to foster love, unity and peace among men.

Difficulties Recognised

95. It realises only too well the enormous difficulties of such a mission. It is well aware of the numerical disproportion between itself and the rest of the human race. It knows its own limitations, its own shortcomings and the failings of its own members. It realises too that the acceptance of the gospel does not depend on any apostolic endeavours of its own, nor on the existence of the right temporal conditions. Faith is a gift of God. He alone determines in the world the order and the time of salvation.

The Church does, however, realise that it is the seed, as it were, the leaven, the salt and the light of the world. Fully conscious of all that is new and remarkable in this modern age, it nevertheless holds its place in a changing world with sincere confidence, and says to men: "Here in my possession is what you are looking for, what you need."

Its promise is to one of earthly happiness, but it does nevertheless provide the best means for the attainment of earthly happiness, namely, light and grace; and it teaches men about their future life which transcends nature. In addition it speaks to them of truth, justice, freedom, progress, concord, civilisation and peace. The Church well knows the value of these things. It knows them in the light of Christ's revelation. It has a message, therefore, for everyone: boys and girls, young men and women, scientists and scholars, working men and men of every class in society, professional men and politicians; but especially the poor, the unfortunate, the sick and the dying - in a word, everybody.

In Terms of Concentric Circles

96. You may say that in making this assertion we are carried away by an excessive zeal for Our office and are not giving sufficient weight to the true position of the Catholic Church vis-a-vis the world. But that is not so. We see the concrete situation very clearly, and might sum it up in general terms by describing it in a series of concentric circles around the central point at which God has placed us.

First Circle: Mankind

97. The first of these circles is immense. Its limits stretch beyond our view into the distant horizon. It comprises the entire human race, the world. We are fully aware of the distance which separates us from the world, but we do not conceive of it as a stranger to us. All things human are our concern. We share with the whole of the human race a common nature, a common life, with all its gifts and all its problems. We are ready to play our part in this primary, universal society, to acknowledge the insistent demands of its fundamental needs, and to applaud the new and often sublime expressions of its genius. But there are moral values of the utmost importance which we have to offer it. These are of advantage to everyone. We root them firmly in the consciences of men. Wherever men are striving to understand themselves and the world, we are able to communicate with them. Wherever the councils of nations come together to establish the rights and duties of man, we are honoured to be permitted to take our place among them. If there is in man a "soul that is naturally Christian," we wish to respect it, to cherish it, and to communicate with it.

98. In all this, as we remind ourselves and others, our attitude is entirely disinterested, devoid of any temporal or political motive. Our sole purpose is to take what is good in man's life on earth and raise it to a supernatural and Christian level. The Church is not identical with civilisation. It does however promote it.

Atheism a Growing Evil

99. Sad to say, this vast circle comprises very many people who profess no religion at all. Many, too, subscribe to atheism in one of its many different forms. They parade their godlessness openly, asserting its claims in education and politics, in the foolish and fatal belief that they are emancipating mankind from false and outworn notions about life and the world and substituting a view that is scientific and up-to-date.

100. This is the most serious problem of our time. We are firmly convinced that the basic propositions of atheism are utterly false and irreconcilable with the underlying principles of thought. They strike at the genuine and effective foundation for man's acceptance of a rational order in the universe, and introduce into human life a futile kind of dogmatism which far from solving life's difficulties, only degrades it and saddens it. Any social system based on these principles is doomed to utter destruction. Atheism, therefore, is not a liberating force, but a catastrophic one, for it seeks to quench the light of the living God. We shall therefore resist this growing evil with all our strength, spurred on by our great zeal for safeguarding the truth, inspired by our social duty of loyally professing Christ and His gospel, and driven on by a burning, unquenchable love, which makes man's good our constant concern. We shall resist in the invincible hope that modern man may recognise the religious ideals which the Catholic faith sets before him and feel himself drawn to seek a form of civilisation which will never fail him but will lead on to the natural and supernatural perfection of the human spirit. May the grace of God enable him to possess his temporal goods in peace and honour and to live in the assurance of acquiring those that are eternal.

Communist Oppression

101. It is for these reasons that We are driven to repudiate such ideologies as deny God and oppress the Church - We repudiate them as Our predecessors did, and as everyone must do who

firmly believes in the excellence and importance of religion. These ideologies are often identified with economic, social and political regimes; atheistic communism is a glaring instance of this. Yet is it really so much we who condemn them? One might say that it is rather they and their politicians who are clearly repudiating us, and for doctrinaire reasons subjecting us to violent oppression. Truth to tell, the voice we raise against them is more the complaint of a victim than the sentence of a judge.

102. In these circumstances dialogue is very difficult, not to say impossible, although we have today no preconceived intention of cutting ourselves off from the adherents of these systems and these regimes. For the lover of truth discussion is always possible. But the difficulties are enormously increased by obstacles of the moral order: by the absence of sufficient freedom of thought and action, and by the calculated misuse of words in debate, so that they serve not the investigation and formulation of objective truth, but purely subjective expediency.

103. Instead of dialogue, therefore, there is silence, for example, the only voice that is heard is the voice of suffering. By its suffering it becomes the mouthpiece of an oppressed and degraded society, deprived by its rulers of every spiritual right. How can a dialogue be conducted in such circumstances as these, even if we embarked upon it? It would be but "a voice crying in the wilderness."[63] The only witness that the Church can give is that of silence, suffering, patience, and unfailing love, and this is a voice that not even death can silence.

Challenge to Understand, Answer, Rectify

104. Though We speak firmly and clearly in defence of religion, and of those human, spiritual values which it proclaims and cherishes, Our pastoral solicitude nevertheless prompts Us to probe into the mind of the modern atheist, in an effort to understand the reasons for his mental turmoil and his denial of God. They are obviously

---

[63] *Mk* 1:3.

many and complex, and we must come to a prudent decision about them, and answer them effectively. They sometimes spring from the demand for a more profound and purer presentation of religious truth, and an objection to forms of language and worship which somehow fall short of the ideal. These things we must remedy. We must do all we can to purify them and make them express more adequately the sacred reality of which they are the signs.

We see these men serving a demanding and often a noble cause, fired with enthusiasm and idealism, dreaming of justice and progress and striving for a social order which they conceive of as the ultimate of perfection, and all but divine. This, for them, is the Absolute and the Necessary. It proves that nothing can tear from their hearts their yearning for God, the first and final cause of all things. It is the task of our teaching Office to reveal to them, with patience and wisdom, that all these things are immanent in human nature and transcend it.

Again we see these men taking pains to work out scientific explanation of the universe by human reasoning, and they are often quite ingenuously enthusiastic about this. It is an enquiry which is all the less reprehensible in that it follows rules of logic very similar to those which are taught in the best schools of philosophy. Such an enquiry, far from providing them, as they suppose, with irrefutable arguments in defence of their atheism, must of its very nature bring them back finally to the metaphysical and logical assertion of the existence of the supreme God.

The atheistic political scientist wilfully stops short at a certain point in this inevitable process of reasoning, and in doing so shuts out the supreme light which gives intelligibility to the universe. Is there no one among us who could help him to arrive at last at the realisation of the objective reality of the cosmic universe which confronts the mind with the presence of God and brings to the lips a healing prayer of tearful humility?

Eventual Dialogue Seen Possible

They are sometimes men of great breadth of mind, impatient with the mediocrity and self-seeking which infects so much of modern society. They are quick to make use of sentiments and expressions found in our Gospel, referring to the brotherhood of man, mutual aid, and human compassion. Shall we not one day be able to lead them back to the Christian sources of these moral values?

105. We would like to recall what Our predecessor Pope John XXIII wrote in his Encyclical *Pacem in Terris.* He drew attention to the fact that although the formulation of a particular philosophy does not change once it has been worked out and systematised, nevertheless the practical programme initiated by such a philosophy is capable of receiving a gradual reorientation, and may in fact undergo considerable changes.[64] We do not therefore give up hope of the eventual possibility of a dialogue between these men and the Church, and a more fruitful one than is possible at present, when we can only express our justifiable complaints and repudiations.

The Cause of Peace

106. Before leaving this subject of the contemporary world, We feel impelled to mention Our cherished hope that this intention of Ours of holding a dialogue and of developing it under all the various and changing aspects which it presents, may assist the cause of peace among men. May it point the way to prudence and sincerity in the ordering of human relationships, and bring experience and wisdom to bear on the problem of recalling all men to the consideration of supernatural values.

The mere fact that we are embarking upon a disinterested, objective and sincere dialogue is a circumstance in favour of a free and honourable peace. It positively excludes all pretence, rivalry, deceit and betrayal. It brands wars of aggression, imperialism, and domination as criminal and catastrophic. It necessarily brings men

[64] Cf. AAS LV (1963), 300.

together on every level: heads of states, the body of the nation and its foundations, whether social, family, or individual. It strives to inspire in every institution and in every soul the understanding and love of peace and the duty to preserve it.

Second Circle: Worshippers of the One God

107. Then we see another circle around us. This too is vast in extent, yet not so far away from us. It comprises first of all those men who worship the one supreme God, whom we also worship. We would mention first the Jewish people, who still retain the religion of the Old Testament, and who are indeed worthy of our respect and love.

Then we have those worshippers who adhere to other monotheistic systems of religion, especially the Moslem religion. We do well to admire these people for all that is good and true in their worship of God.

And finally we have the followers of the great Afro-Asiatic religions. Obviously we cannot agree with these various forms of religion, nor can we adopt an indifferent or uncritical attitude toward them on the assumption that they are all to be regarded as on an equal footing, and that there is no need for those who profess them to enquire whether or not God has Himself revealed definitively and infallibly how He wishes to be known, loved, and served. Indeed, honesty compels us to declare openly our conviction that the Christian religion is the one and only true religion, and it is our hope that it will be acknowledged as such by all who look for God and worship Him.

Common Ideals in Many Spheres

108. But we do not wish to turn a blind eye to the spiritual and moral values of the various non-Christian religions, for we desire to join with them in promoting and defending common ideals in the spheres of religious liberty, human brotherhood, education, culture, social welfare, and civic order. Dialogue is possible in all these great projects, which are our concern as much as theirs, and

we will not fail to offer opportunities for discussion in the event of such an offer being favourably received in genuine, mutual respect.

Third Circle: Christians

109. And so we come to the circle which is nearest to us, and which comprises all those who take their name from Christ. In this area the ecumenical dialogue, as it is called, is already in being, and there are places where it is beginning to make considerable progress. There is much more that could be said on this complex and delicate matter, but this will not be Our final word on the subject. So for the moment We will merely refer in passing to a few fairly obvious points.

Ready to Meet Legitimate Desires

We readily accept the principle of stressing what we all have in common rather than what divides us. This provides a good and fruitful basis for our dialogue, and we are prepared to engage upon it with a will. We would even go further and declare our readiness to examine how we can meet the legitimate desires of our separated Christian brothers on many points of difference concerning tradition, spirituality, canon law, and worship, for it is Our dearest wish to embrace them in a perfect union of faith and charity.

We must stress however that it is not in Our power to make any concessions regarding the integrity of the faith and the obligations of charity. We realise that this may cause misgiving and opposition in certain quarters, but now that the Catholic Church has on its own initiative taken steps to restore the unity of Christ's fold, it will not cease to exercise the greatest prudence and deliberation. It will continue to insist that the claims it makes for itself - claims which still have the effect of alienating the separated brethren - derive from the will of Christ, not from any spirit of self-aggrandisement based on the record of its past achievements, nor from any unsound theological speculation. Rightly understood, they will be seen to be for the good of all, for the common unity, liberty and fullness of the Christian life. The Catholic Church will never cease to prepare itself by prayer and penance for the longed-for reconciliation.

Papacy an Apparent Obstacle

110. That We, who promote this reconciliation, should be regarded by many of Our separated brothers as an obstacle to it, is a matter of deep distress to Us. The obstacle would seem to be the primacy of honour and jurisdiction which Christ bestowed on the Apostle Peter, and which We have inherited as his Successor.

But Principle of Unity

Are there not those who say that unity between the separated Churches and the Catholic Church would be more easily achieved if the primacy of the Roman pontiff were done away with? We beg our separated brothers to consider the groundlessness of this opinion. Take away the sovereign Pontiff and the Catholic Church would no longer be catholic. Moreover, without the supreme, effective, and authoritative pastoral office of Peter the unity of Christ's Church would collapse. It would be vain to look for other principles of unity in place of the true one established by Christ Himself. As St Jerome rightly observed: "There would be as many schisms in the Church as there are priests."[65]

And Primacy of Service and Love

We would add that this cardinal principle of holy Church is not a supremacy of spiritual pride and a desire to dominate mankind, but a primacy of service, ministration, and love. It is no vapid rhetoric which confers on Christ's vicar the title: "Servant of the servants of God".

111. These then are the lines of our dialogue. But before we engage in conversation with our brothers, we address ourselves lovingly to our Heavenly Father in earnest prayer and great confidence.

[65] Cf. Dial. *contra Luciferianos*, n. 9; PL 23. 173.

Reunion Held Promising

112. It is a source of joy and hope to Us, Venerable Brethren, to note the spiritual fervour that is being aroused in this varied and wide circle of Christians. For this would seem to augur well for the future unification of all Christians in the one Church of Christ.

We pray for the breath of the Holy Spirit on the ecumenical movement, and recall once more the emotion and joy We felt in Jerusalem at our meeting with the Patriarch Athenagoras. It was a meeting that abounded in charity, and fired Us with new hope. We welcome with gratitude and respect those representatives of the separated churches who are taking part in the Second Vatican Ecumenical Council. We assure them once again of Our enthusiastic and attentive interest in all those spiritual movements concerned or connected with the problem of unity which are stirring individuals, groups, and communities noted for their noble piety. We greet all these Christians with love and reverence, confident that the cause of Christ and the unity which He Himself willed for His Church will be promoted by our sincere and friendly dialogue.

Last Circle: Catholics

113. We address Ourself finally to the sons of God's house, the one, holy, Catholic, and apostolic Church of which the Roman Church is "mother and head." How greatly we desire that this dialogue with Our own children may be conducted with the fullness of faith, with charity, and with dynamic holiness. May it be of frequent occurrence and on an intimate level. May it be open and responsive to all truth, every virtue, every spiritual value that goes to make us the heritage of Christian teaching. We want it to be sincere. We want it to be an inspiration to genuine holiness. We want it to show itself ready to listen to the variety of views which are expressed in the world today. We want it to be the sort of dialogue that will make Catholics virtuous, wise, unfettered, fair-minded and strong.

Obedience Still to be Exercised

114. But this desire that the Church's internal relationships should take the form of a dialogue between members of a community founded upon love, does not mean that the virtue of obedience is no longer operative. The right to command and the duty to obey must be present in any properly constituted society, especially in the Church which is structured on a sacred hierarchy. Its authority was established by Christ. It is His representative, the authoritative organ of His Word, the expression of His great pastoral love. Hence obedience has faith as its starting point. It is exercised in the school of evangelical humility. It is a participation in the wisdom, unity, idealism, and charity which are ruling factors in the corporate life of the Church. It confers upon him who commands and upon him who obeys the merit of being like Christ who "was made obedient even unto death."[66]

115. Moreover the very exercise of authority becomes, in the context of this dialogue, an exercise of obedience, the obedient performance of a service, a ministry of truth and charity. By obedience We mean the observance of canonical regulations and respect for the government of lawful superiors, but an observance and respect readily and serenely given, as is only to be expected from free and loving children.

By contrast, a spirit of independence, bitter criticism, defiance, and arrogance is far removed from that charity which nourishes and preserves the spirit of fellowship, harmony, and peace in the Church. It completely vitiates dialogue, turning it into argument, disagreement and dissension - a sad state of affairs, but by no means uncommon. St Paul warned us against this when he said: "Let there be no schisms among you."[67]

---

[66] *Ph* 2:8.

[67] *1 Co* 1:10.

A Fine Beginning - A Long Way to Go

116. It is Our keen desire therefore that this dialogue which has long been engaging the attention of the Church may take on a new inspiration, new themes, and new speakers, and thereby increase the holiness and vitality of the Mystical Body of Christ on earth.

We give Our unhesitating support to anything which can help to spread the teaching of those truths of which the Church is guardian and minister. We have already mentioned the liturgy and preaching as forming the basis of the interior life. We would also mention schools, the press, the social apostolate, the missions, and works of charity. All these are things which the Ecumenical Council will doubtless bring up for our discussion. We bless and encourage all who, under the guidance of competent authority, take part in the Church's vital, health-giving dialogue. We are thinking particularly of Our priests, religious, and Our well-beloved laity who are fighting for Christ in the ranks of Catholic Action and in the other associations and activities of the apostolate.

117. We rejoice and find great consolation in the fact that this dialogue, both inside and outside the Church, has already begun. The Church today is more alive than ever before. But when we weigh the matter more closely we see that there is still a great way to go. In fact the work which is beginning today will never come to an end. This is a law of our earthly, time-bound pilgrimage. It is, Venerable Brethren, the common condition of that ministry of ours which everything today urges us to renew and undertake with greater alacrity and devotion.

118. As for Ourself, in speaking to you of these things We are glad not only to rely on your co-operation, but also to offer Our own in return. We ask for and We promise this union of aims and activities just one year after Our accession to the throne of Peter and Our assumption of the name and also, please God, something of the spirit, of the Apostle of the Gentiles.

119. And so We end this Our first encyclical on a note of great joy in the union of our spirits which has its origin in Christ. As your father and brother We bestow upon you, in the name of the immortal God, Our apostolic blessing, and gladly extend it to the whole Church and to all mankind.

Given at St Peter's, Rome, on the Feast of the Transfiguration of Our Lord Jesus Christ, the sixth day of August, in the year 1964, the second of Our Pontificate.

PAUL VI